THIS IS
BORNEO

THIS IS
BORNEO

Text by Junaidi Payne
Photographs by Gerald Cubitt and Dennis Lau

Preface by David J. Bellamy
Consultant: Jayl Langub

NEW
HOLLAND

Produced in association with WWF Malaysia

First published in the UK in 1994 by
New Holland (Publishers) Ltd
37 Connaught Street, London W2 2AZ

ISBN 1 85368 329 9

Commissioning Editor: Charlotte Parry-Crooke
Project Manager: Tim Jollands
Editors: Ann Baggaley and Beverley Jollands
Designer: Philip Mann, ACE Limited
Cartography: Julian Baker
Index: Beverley Jollands

Reproduction by Scantrans, Singapore
Printed and bound in Malaysia by Times Offset (M) Sdn. Bhd.

CONTENTS

PHOTOGRAPHIC ACKNOWLEDGEMENTS

The publishers extend their thanks to the following individuals and organizations who kindly
loaned their photographs for inclusion in this book. All the photographs in the book,
with the exception of those listed below, were taken by Gerald Cubitt.

Dennis Lau: page 12, page 13, page 16, page 22, pages 35 to 39, pages 41 to 50

Jack Jackson: page 92 (above left), page 166 to 168, page 170 (above), page 171

Debbie Martyr: page 94 (below), page 103 (below), page 113

Junaidi Payne: page 85 (below), page 95 (centre right), page 119 (below), page 120,
page 121 (below), page 122 (below), page 132 (bottom), page 135 (top)

Cede Prudente: page 129, page 140, page 145, page 148, page 152 (above left), page 158 (below)

R. Rajanathan: page 95 (bottom right), page 149 (below)

Royal Geographical Society/Brunei Rainforest Project
Chris Caldicott: page 70, page 71 (above), pages 72 to 75 • Paul Harris: page 58 (below left), page 71 (below)

Sabah Museum/Woolley Collection: page 18, page 32, page 53
Sabah Museum/ Martin and Osa Johnson Collection: page 33

Sabah Parks: page 76 (above left)

Sabah State Archives: page 31

Secret Sea Visions (Burt Jones and Maurine Shimlock): page 138 (below left), page 169 (right), page 170 (below)

WWF Malaysia Photolibrary: page 95 (bottom left)
Lena Chan: page 118 (below) • Andy Johns: page 153 (below) • Mikaail Kavanagh: page 152 (below)
Rodney Lai: page 152 (above right) • Junaidi Payne: page 132 (top), page 135 (centre)
R. Rajanathan: page 123 (below), page 128 (below centre), page 135 (bottom)

Sylvia Yorath: page 87 (above), page 118 (above), page 128 (above and below left), page 132 (centre)

Illustrations appearing in the preliminary pages are as follows:
HALF TITLE: Iban dancer, Sarawak.
FRONTISPIECE: Tropical island off Semporna, Sabah.
TITLE PAGE: Young Orang-utan, Tanjung Puting National Park, Central Kalimantan.
PAGE 4: Segama River, Sabah.
PAGE 5: Santubong beach, Sarawak.
PAGE 7: Floating market, Banjarmasin, South Kalimantan.
PAGE 10: Gunung Kinabalu, viewed from Kota Kinabalu, Sabah.
PAGE 11: Sarawak River at Kuching, Sarawak.
BELOW: Omar Ali Saifuddin Mosque, Bandar Seri Begawan, Brunei Darussalam.

ACKNOWLEDGEMENTS

Interest in this project has been forthcoming from numerous sources around the world. The publishers would especially like to thank the sponsors, contributors and consultants for their involvement. The author, photographers and publishers would like to express their gratitude to the following for their generous and valuable assistance during the preparation of this book:

World Wide Fund For Nature (WWF) Malaysia
Malaysia Tourism Promotion Board, Ministry of Culture, Arts & Tourism
Ministry of Environment & Tourism, Sarawak
Development & Commercial Bank Berhad
Perlis Plantations Berhad
Rashid Hussain Berhad
Shell Companies in Malaysia
Sime Darby Group

WWF MALAYSIA
Dr Mikaail Kavanagh, Executive Director
Susan Abraham • Dr Isabelle Louis • Christina Yin • Sabri Zain

MALAYSIA
Sabah Forestry Department • Sabah Foundation
Sabah Ministry of Tourism and Environment Development
Sabah Parks • Sabah Wildlife Department
National Parks and Wildlife Office, Sarawak Forestry Department
Communities of Sandakan, Kota Kinabalu and the Kinabatangan River
Saimon Ambi • Ron Holland, Borneo Divers
David Labang • Tony and Anthea Lamb
Francis Liew, Sabah Parks
Malaysia Airlines
Holiday Inn, Kuching • Hyatt Kinabalu International

INDONESIA
Joop Avé, Minister of Tourism
Andi Mappisammeng, Director-General of Tourism, Indonesia
Drs Effendy Sumardja and the Central and Field Staff of
the Offices of Natural Resources and Nature Conservation
Udin Saifuddin, Marketing Director, Directorate General of Tourism
Peter Pangaribuan and Zain Sumedy, Directorate General of Tourism
Garuda Indonesia • Merpati Nusantara Airlines

Special thanks also go to:
Professor David J. Bellamy
Ken Scriven
The Earl of Cranbrook • Nigel de N. Winser
Janet Cubitt • Azizah Hamid
Glyn Davies • Jack Jackson • Dr Kathy MacKinnon
William Rivière
The Royal Geographical Society

SULU SEA

SEPILOK
FOREST
RESERVE

TURTLE ISLANDS
PARK

Sandakan

Sandakan Bay

OMANTONG

Segaliud

KULAMBA
WILDLIFE RESERVE

TAPADONG

Kinabatangan

Lahad TABIN
Datu WILDLIFE RESERVE

Segama

Tungku

VALLEY

Sapagaya

Silam

Darvel Bay

MADAI

SEMPORNA
ISLANDS

TURONGO

AWAU HILLS PARK

Semporna

Tawau

PULAU
SEBATIK

PULAU
SIPADAN

SULAWESI
SEA

Tarakan

Tanjungselor

PULAU
MARATUA

jungredeb

gkulirang

NAL PARK

Bontang

arong

Samarinda

ariset-Samboja
arch Station

apan

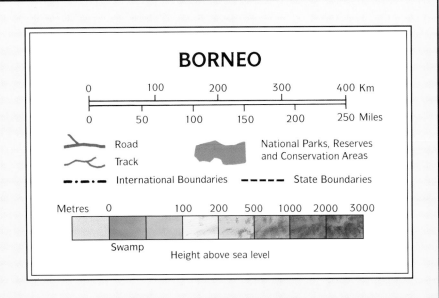

BORNEO

	0	100	200	300	400 Km
0	50	100	150	200	250 Miles

Road

Track

National Parks, Reserves
and Conservation Areas

International Boundaries   State Boundaries

Metres   0   100   200   500   1000   2000   3000

Swamp   Height above sea level

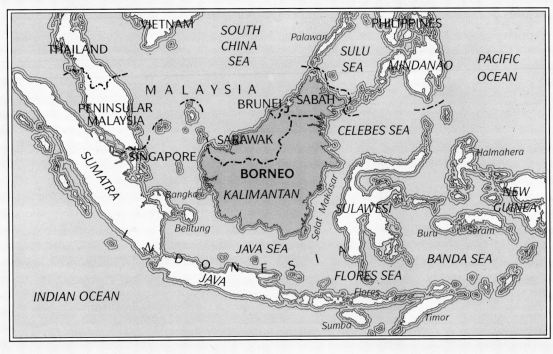

VIETNAM

THAILAND

SOUTH
CHINA
SEA

Palawan

PHILIPPINES

SULU
SEA

MINDANAO

PACIFIC
OCEAN

M A L A Y S I A

PENINSULAR
MALAYSIA

BRUNEI SABAH

CELEBES SEA

Halmahera

SARAWAK

SINGAPORE

SUMATRA

Bangka

BORNEO

KALIMANTAN

Selat Makasar

SULAWESI

NEW
GUINEA

Buru

Seram

Belitung

JAVA SEA

BANDA SEA

I N D O N E S I A

JAVA

FLORES SEA

INDIAN OCEAN

Flores

Sumba

Timor

PREFACE

Seven hundred and forty thousand square kilometres of tropical island sitting astride the equator, home to a great diversity of people, plants and animals which once and not all that long ago lived sustainably, part of the rainforests and coral reefs of the Island of Borneo: I first came to know about this, the third largest island in the world, while reading the adventures of the Victorian naturalist Alfred Russel Wallace.

His general studies of the diverse animal life of the region led him to draw a hypothetical line separating the Oriental and the Australasian fauna. Today with our understanding of continental drift we would call these the fauna of the two supercontinents Laurasia and Gondwanaland, a fauna all set about with old growth forests, home of the largest flower in the world.

I just had to go and see it for myself and from the cloud forests of Gunung Kinabalu, through the limestone country of Mulu and the unique peat swamp forests to the depths of the diverse reefs, it lives up to every expectation.

This is a tropical paradise by any definition of the term.

Unfortunately, like all such places the world over, the treasures of Borneo have come under massive attack especially during the last thirty years.

This excellent and timely book draws on pictures from the past, experiences from the present, and looks to the future in which the governments and people of Brunei, Indonesia and Malaysia could show the world the way towards sustainability once again.

David J. Bellamy
The Conservation Foundation
London

FOREWORD

For those who live outside the South-east Asian region and have accumulated an image of Borneo gleaned from magazine articles and television documentaries, the picture is out of focus. Borneo would appear to be a massive steamy forest, inhabited by noisy birds, Orang-utans and exotic tribespeople, under threat from irresponsible loggers who are determined to destroy the forests, with the world's wealthiest man, the Sultan of Brunei, living on the coast.

To those of us who live here, Borneo is simply home. If asked to list what we consider to be the main features of our home country, whichever part of Borneo we come from, our replies might indicate feelings of living in a developing country, where physical changes, steadily improving infrastructure, new opportunities, and hopes of improved standards of living are high on the list. Some might express concern over logging and deforestation, but we could probably also point out that Borneo still has a lot more forest than most other regions in the world.

This is Borneo has been produced in close collaboration with the World Wide Fund For Nature (WWF) Malaysia, an organization which, as a matter of policy, always attempts to take a balanced, factual approach in its conservation work. Thus, the book provides a balanced view of the world's third largest island, using a unique blend of photographs and succinct yet wide-ranging text that encompasses natural history, geography, history, government, people, economic changes and conservation issues.

YM Tengku D.Z. Adlin
Trustee
WWF Malaysia

11

PROFILE OF BORNEO

Borneo is the third largest island in the world after Greenland and New Guinea. A vast green tropical wilderness, set within the sprawling Malaysian-Indonesian archipelago, it straddles the equator over an area of nearly 740,000 square kilometres (285,714 square miles), enfringed by tropical seas and a scattering of coral reefs.

The scale of this rugged and stunningly beautiful land – thrust upwards by mountains, heavily clad in forest and dissected by mighty silt-laden rivers – is immense. An unrivalled wealth of natural life includes some of the world's most extraordinarily varied plants and animals, many of which are found only in Borneo, and the potential for new discoveries is never-ending. Perhaps above all, Borneo's fascination lies in the multicultural diversity of its many peoples, who may remain true to their individual ethnic origins yet together characterize the land that they share.

Having emerged from a tangled web of historical circumstances, present-day Borneo is divided between three nations – Brunei Darussalam (commonly abbreviated to Brunei), Malaysia and Indonesia. In the north-west, the tiny independent sultanate of Brunei, established in early times as a centre of power and trade, covers a mere 5,765 square kilometres (2,226 square miles). The capital is the pleasant modern city of Bandar Seri Begawan. Brunei is surrounded and, indeed, divided into two separate territories by Sarawak, Malaysia's largest state, occupying 123,985 square kilometres (47,870 square miles) and representing the area of land acquired by the English Brooke family from the Sultan of Brunei during the 19th century. The name of the capital, Kuching, means 'cat' in Malay. Legend has it that the site of the original town was famed for its *mata kuching* (cat's eyes) trees, which bear shiny, round, edible fruits. Sabah, the second largest Malaysian state, 73,620 square kilometres (28,425 square miles), occupies Borneo's northernmost tip and was once a possession of a British trading company, which bought the territory from the sultans of Brunei and Sulu in the late 19th century. Kota Kinabalu, the capital, is named after Sabah's famous Gunung (Mount) Kinabalu. Both Sabah and Sarawak constitute 'East' Malaysia, set apart from Peninsular or 'West' Malaysia by the expanse of the South China Sea.

The remainder of Borneo, and by far the largest portion, belongs to Indonesia. This huge region, Kalimantan, where once the Dutch strove to assert their sovereignty, covers a total area of 535,834 square kilometres (206,886 square miles) and is divided into four administrative provinces: East Kalimantan (known as Kalimantan Timur in Indonesian), probably once the ancient kingdom of Mulawarman, with the provincial capital at Samarinda; South Kalimantan (Kalimantan Selatan), originally the Muslim sultanate of Banjar, as the name of the capital city – Banjarmasin – recalls; Central Kalimantan (Kalimantan Tengah),

---

created in 1957 to settle internecine conflict, with its capital at Palangkaraya; and West Kalimantan (Kalimantan Barat), consisting mainly of the catchment area of the Kapuas, Indonesia's longest river, on the banks of which the capital, Pontianak, was founded in the 1770s.

For centuries, the lure of Borneo's mysterious depths drew explorers, traders and adventurers in search of the bizarre, the exotic and the sensational. The myths that once excited such interest have been left behind in the past, where they belong, but the island holds no less attraction for the present-day traveller. Modern communications have opened up the routes to much that once lay hidden from all but the most intrepid. Today, the visitor can journey to the rainforests of the interior with comparative ease to look at wildlife or find an older style of life. Well-established national parks and reserves offer the chance to see such specialities as the Orang-utan or collections of rare orchids, and a developing tourist industry operates both inland and around the coral-rich offshore diving sites that are becoming increasingly accessible.

THE LAND

In the distant past, Borneo and many of the other islands which now constitute Indonesia, including Sumatra, were connected to the Asian continent in an enormous land mass. As sea levels rose at the end of the last Ice Age, these links were severed, leaving Borneo isolated in shallow waters and anchored on the submerged extension of mainland Asia known as the Sunda Shelf. The ancient connections are still reflected in similarities in the plants and animals of Borneo and the Asian mainland.

Yet, when considered in geological time spans, Borneo is a young land, the bulk of the island consisting of great layers of sedimentary rocks that have mostly built up under the sea during the past 60 million years. Movements of the earth's surface have caused the layers of rocks to become jumbled, folded and exposed. Igneous and metamorphic rocks, which have their origins far below the vast layers of sediments, protrude in scattered localities throughout the island, forming mountains, hill ranges and isolated outcrops. The most spectacular of

these upheavals is Gunung Kinabalu in west Sabah, at 4,101 metres (13,455 feet) the highest mountain not only in Borneo but in the entire South-east Asian region. It is an immense and impressive feature, its jagged topmost peaks breaking free of the blanketing tree cover to tower above the surrounding ranges. Gunung Kinabalu's mass of granite was pushed up through the surface of the earth only about 1.5 million years ago, and it is still slowly rising. There has been no volcanic activity in Borneo, however, for over 20,000 years.

Borneo's coastline is gradually changing. In some areas, sea currents carry sand, continuously altering the configurations of the beautiful white beaches, but the process of coastal formation is far more evident where large rivers empty into the sea. Here, tons of silt become trapped and rapidly colonized by the pervasive mangrove vegetation as it reaches ever forwards. Behind the swamps begin the forests that smother the contours of the land.

From the steep mountainous spine that stretches from the tip of Sabah in the north, splaying out across the island almost to the coast of West Kalimantan, a network of rivers descends in all directions, constantly swollen by the heavy annual rainfall. These waterways are the main arteries of Borneo, over the centuries allowing communication and shifts of settlement deep in the interior and giving birth to the towns and cities that have sprung up around the island's perimeter where riverbanks widen on the approach to the sea.

BORNEO'S CLIMATE

The entire island of Borneo lies within the equatorial zone. Temperatures are high throughout the year. In the lowlands, daytime temperatures average 30℃ (86°F), while a night-time temperature of 20℃ (68°F) is considered cold near the coast. There is roughly a 1℃ (1.8°F) drop in average temperature for every 90 metres (300 feet) increase in elevation above sea level. Annual rainfall is high throughout Borneo, but there are surprising variations in both the amount and pattern in different regions of the island. For example, interior plains surrounded by mountains typically receive under 2,000 millimetres (80 inches), evenly spaced through the year, while some of the mountainous areas of Sarawak receive over 5,000 millimetres (200 inches) annually. Rainfall patterns in northern and western Borneo are affected by the monsoon winds of the South Asian region, which tend to bring heavy rains around November to February and May to June. To minimize the risk of hitting a rainy period and also to have a chance of coinciding with a flowering or fruiting season, the periods February to April and August to September are generally best for visiting most parts of Borneo.

THE PLANT LIFE OF BORNEO

Except in a few circumstances – such as on steep rocky land and in areas of intensive human activity – the natural vegetation of Borneo is tropical rainforest. This suggests to the imagination a uniform mass of dense, dark, humid jungle but, in fact, there is an enormous variation in the pattern and type of growth. Natural factors, such as soil and water, obviously have the most influence but, increasingly, humans are responsible for the greatest changes to the appearance, condition and extent of Bornean forests.

'Old growth' or 'primary' forests – which may never have been cleared, or were perhaps cleared a very long time ago – are tall, generally containing a diversity of plant species and a wide range of tree sizes varying from spindly saplings to mature giants with trunks more than 3 metres (10 feet) in circumference. Little sunlight penetrates the spreading canopies of the highest trees and in the green gloom of the lower storeys, relished only by certain shade-loving species, younger trees struggle for existence. 'Secondary' forests, which have grown up after a previous forest has been cleared or destroyed completely are typically of lower stature. Although more open and less oppressive in atmosphere, they contain fewer plant and animal species. In 'logged' forests, where usually only large trees from old growth are felled and removed, sunlit clearings give smaller trees, saplings and seedlings a chance to grow.

Even where there is no human activity, natural occurrences such as disease, wind, rain and landslips have a significant effect. A small percentage of trees in Bornean old growth forests die each year and occasion-ally large gaps are torn open during storms. The result is a patchwork of vegetation cover. Most of the forest may be counted as mature, containing massive trees, some hundreds of years old, well into their prime and often beyond it. This is interspersed with a few gaps left by tree falls within recent months or years and quite a large proportion of 'building-phase' vegetation, where immature trees are growing as secondary forest in gaps left by old tree falls.

This variety in structure of the old growth forests is a key factor in maintaining the diversity of wildlife. The holes and cracks in huge old trees serve as sleeping and breeding sites for flying squirrels, porcupines, hornbills and lizards. Fallen trees provide habitats for fungi, termites, beetles and other invertebrate animals. These creatures in turn provide food for treeshrews and ground squirrels, which can be glimpsed scampering around throughout the day. Building-phase forest often seems to be favoured by monkeys and ground-dwelling birds such as partridges, pheasants and pittas.

A Hidden World beneath the Trees

In the stillness and shade of the forest floor, where the energy-giving rays of the sun barely reach, a complicated and finely balanced ecosystem is at work. Much of it is hidden from sight but without it growth could not be sustained and the forests would fail.

Vital to this system are the fungi that grow in profusion throughout the rainforests and take a multitude of forms. Some appear as mushrooms, at least for part of their life cycle, pushing up from the forest floor or sprouting from fallen trees. Often extraordinarily beautiful and vividly coloured, they range from the typical domed 'toadstool' to shapes resembling intricate fans or bright branching corals. Some glow with eerie luminescence in the black of night. Others are invisible in leaf litter or under the ground. Many play a crucial role in breaking down dead vegetation and in helping to maintain soil condition. In addition, because most tropical soils are shallow and poor in nutrients, living plants depend on soil-dwelling fungi for their very existence. These fungi, known as *mycorrhizae*, are dispersed through the leaf-litter and soil by small animals such as forest rats and form close physical relationships with the roots of plants. Extending themselves, and effectively the root systems, through the soil in a fine network of threads they are able to bring water and scarce minerals to their host plant.

It is astonishing not only that such an array of luxuriant plants can be maintained by this delicate biological life-chain but that forest trees have such a precarious hold on the soil. Even for massive specimens nearly 60 metres (200 feet) high, most of the roots lie amazingly close to the surface. This becomes obvious at recent tree falls where, at the bottom end, just a shallow depression can be seen in the ground. These depressions trap rainwater and form perfect wallows for wild pigs and breeding pools for forest-dwelling frogs. In a seeming attempt to counteract their top-heaviness many trees develop root buttresses at the base of the trunk. These huge woody flanges, which appear to prop up the towering giant above, are one of the striking features of the Bornean rainforest.

A Botanical Paradise

Borneo can be regarded as a botanical garden on a grand scale, with a collection of some of the rarest, most exotic and most prolific plants on earth.

Without doubt, trees make the landscape. Over 3,000 species have been recorded from Borneo and new discoveries are still being made. Mature trees of some species grow to between 45 and 75 metres (150 and 250 feet) in height, and over 3 metres (10 feet) in circumference, though the majority are much smaller. In some forests, more than 400 tree species may be found in just one hectare (2.5 acres). Superficially they may look similar, but they vary in many ways – for example, in the texture and colour of their wood and bark.

Over most of Borneo's land area, a single plant family, the Dipterocarpaceae, dominates the forest in terms of numbers and size of trees. For animals, the dipterocarps do not provide much in the way of food, but they are vital for some species in providing a means by which to travel through the forest, to escape danger and to sleep or nest. Gibbons, squirrels, lizards, even snakes, can swing, leap or glide

between the closely massed branches at surprising speed.

More useful as food plants to Bornean animals are members of the legume or bean family, some of which grow as large trees and others as woody climbing plants. Most Bornean trees bear rather small, inconspicuous flowers and hard, bitter fruits inedible to humans, but there are also wild fruit trees with potential to be selected and brought into cultivation. For example, 24 wild mango species, 25 wild breadfruits and 19 wild durians are known to occur in Borneo. Some of these trees can be seen fairly easily in places like the forest reserve at the Ulu Dusun Agricultural Research Station near Sandakan in Sabah.

Many plants in the forest make use of trees as supports, winding in relentless spirals around trunks and dangling in matted webs from branches. These climbers include woody lianas and the spiny palms known as rattans. The latter have played a role in rural craftsmanship for centuries, their stems being woven into baskets, furniture and other decorative ware, much of which now has popular appeal in the export market. A highly distinctive woody plant which is neither a tree nor a liana is the strangling fig. These stranglers, as they are often called, start life as a small seed, deposited in the dropping of a bird or mammal on the branch of a tall tree. As the strangler grows it gradually encloses its host in massive festoons of aerial roots that frequently strangle the host to death. The fig fruits and leaf shoots provide food for numerous forest creatures.

Of all Bornean plants, the orchids are the best known and also the most diverse. Over 2,500 species, in a bewildering variety of glorious colours and shapes, have been identified and the list is by no means complete. A few grow on the ground but most species are epiphytes – growing on the surfaces of other plants, mainly trees. Some of the most beautiful orchids are the rarest,

and are endangered through collection for international markets and loss of their essential forest habitat. The main area to see orchids is around Gunung Kinabalu, though in the rainforest their exquisitely delicate flowers can sometimes be overlooked. However, visitors can admire the world's finest collection of lowland Bornean orchids at the Tenom Agricultural Research Station in Sabah, where rare species are tended to guard against extinction in the wild.

Other epiphytes in the forests include ferns and, in shady parts of the forest floor, various herbaceous species thrive among the bewildering array of vegetation, often of great beauty when seen at close range. Plants of the Araceae family form a prominent group, with attractive fleshy heart-shaped leaves that give them great potential for development as cultivated ornamentals. Another group, the gingers, are also attracting the attention of botanists. Over 160 Bornean species have been described, many believed to possess value not only as ornamentals but for use in medicines, industrial chemicals and flavourings.

In forests where the soils are exceptionally poor in nutrients, and especially in the higher areas, the unique pitcher plants may be found. These curious species bear an elongated structure like a decorated cup – in fact a modified form of leaf-tip – filled with liquid to trap unwary insects, which the plants then digest.

The wealth of forest plants in Borneo possesses great value which is difficult to measure precisely in monetary terms. Such commodities as timber and rattan are among the top economic products of Borneo but many wild fruits, orchids, other ornamentals and medicinal plants never enter the markets, and their value lies as much in the potential for future cultivation and improvement as in present use. Equally important but impossible to quantify is the fact that, together, forest plants act to maintain soil quality and moderate natural erosion processes. Perhaps the true importance of the tropical rainforests, with their staggering variety of genes, chemical compounds and complex ecological systems, lies in their function as an enormous natural library and research laboratory. The Bornean rainforest helps to maintain the stability of the global atmosphere, absorb-

ing carbon dioxide and releasing oxygen. Locally, the forest contributes to the functioning of the water cycle, absorbing ground water and pumping out water vapour that forms clouds and rain.

A DIVERSITY OF HABITATS

Between coasts and highlands, the broad sweep of Borneo's landscape passes through many changes of character. Swamps give way to alluvial lowlands, gigantic rainforests clothe the slopes as the hills lift upwards, and as the land becomes steeper the tree canopy diminishes until only moss-tufted bushes remain to cluster round the base of the final rocky peaks. These zones are distinguished by their different types of soil and vegetation, and by the wildlife that each supports.

The Coastal Zone

Most of Borneo's coastline consists of either sandy beaches or muddy swamps; cliffs and rocky shorelines are relatively scarce and localized. One of the best and most accessible examples of protected rocky coast is the beautiful Bako National Park not far from Kuching in Sarawak, which contains a remarkable range of habitats.

On bare sandy shores exposed to salt spray and the relentless heat of the tropical seaside sun, only a few tree species are able to colonize successfully. One of these is the attractive Aru, superficially resembling a conifer, which is useful in helping to stabilize those shores still being deposited by sea currents, and in providing shade. On stable and eroding sandy coasts, the natural vegetation is dense, low tree cover, often dominated by another attractive tree, the Putat Laut. Above the beaches, among the dunes, the tough, fibrous Screw-pine sometimes grows. The fibres from the long thick leaves of this plant are used for making mats, sacks and baskets, though with the availability of synthetic materials this practice is becoming outdated. Examples of protected sandy beach vegetation can be seen in all the island parks in Sabah and at Similajau National Park in Sarawak.

Sandy beaches in parts of Borneo and on some of the offshore islands are the nesting grounds of sea turtles. Two species in particular – the Green and Hawksbill –

Opposite: A Penan man in traditional hunting gear. He carries a dual-purpose blowpipe with spear, quiver of poisoned darts and parang (knife). Only a very few Penan follow an entirely hunting and gathering style of life nowadays.

17

come ashore during the night and, scooping holes with their flippers, lay upwards of 80 eggs per clutch. Collection of the eggs by people over many generations, coupled with increasing human use of the coastal zone in general, has led to a serious reduction in the numbers of these turtles. The major known sea turtle nesting beaches are now those on a few islands off north-eastern Borneo. Small sandy islands off Sabah are also home to the rare Dusky Scrubfowl, a bird that lays its eggs in mounds of sand and rotting vegetation, leaving them to be incubated by natural heat.

Muddy areas of the coast which are periodically inundated with sea-water are typically covered with mangrove forests. Mangroves are among the youngest of all tropical forests because they exist within a zone which is slowly but constantly changing. Small changes in sea level or in deposition of sediments, for example, can kill mangrove forests in one place while opening up new areas elsewhere for colonization. The trees in this humid, watery world consist of a few species only, specially adapted to survive in their unstable environment. Many have peculiar aerial roots, either in the form of curved stilts which grow out from the trunk, or spikes which grow up out

of the mud. These arrangements may provide support but it is believed that their main function is to allow the trees' root systems to absorb and release gases in the otherwise airless environment of water-logged mud.

At first glance, mangroves seem to be forbidding and inhospitable but, in fact, they are rich in many forms of animal life. Fiddler crabs and the curious mudskipper fishes which, with the aid of their front fins, skip across the surface of the mud and on to the lower parts of trees, are distinctive and readily seen mangrove inhabitants. In some locations, fireflies congregate on the trees at night and emit simultaneous flashes of light. And in the murky waters a large variety of fish and prawn species find food and shelter.

Mangrove wood is hard, and is used for the supports of houses built over the sea, for piling, construction of fish traps, as firewood and for production of charcoal. The bark of some species is rich in tannin and this substance was extracted on a commercial scale in Borneo and exported for tanning purposes, under the name of 'Borneo cutch', in the late 19th to early 20th centuries, a period when leather, ropes and string from natural fibres were still important worldwide.

Tamu *at Tuaran, Sabah, around 1915.*
This traditional market is still held every Sunday in this small coastal town.

Mangrove forests are generally in good condition in Borneo, but in some localities they are under threat from intensive wood harvesting, from conversion to aquaculture ponds and from being regarded as useless land suitable only for infilling or waste disposal. Small samples of mangroves can be seen by walking in Tunku Abdul Rahman Park in Sabah or Bako National Park in Sarawak, but only a boat trip in extensive mangrove forests – for example in Brunei Bay or east of Sandakan in Sabah – can convey the true atmosphere of this habitat.

Where sea-water mixes with the fresh water brought down through the swamps by rivers, stands of the Nipa palm typically develop. Nipa, which consists of a massive, trunkless rosette of leaf fronds, occurs profusely along riverbanks near the sea and between mangrove and inland swamps. The leaves were used extensively for roof thatching in coastal areas of Borneo and still are in some areas. Such roofs, commonly known as *atap*, last for at least two years before needing replacement. In many fishing communities, the walls of houses are also traditionally made of Nipa leaves. The outer skin of young leaves is peeled off and cut into cigarette papers, which may be seen on sale in small bundles at village markets, for use with locally grown tobacco. The young seeds of Nipa are gathered and cooked by some coastal communities to provide a pleasant nutty food. The kernels of unripe Nipa seeds – resembling a cross between a jelly-baby and a nut – may be eaten as a snack.

When flowers are developing on a Nipa there is a flow of sweet sap in the flower stalk; this was, and in some places still is, tapped to produce a treacly sugar, an alcoholic drink, or vinegar. In 1924, the government of North Borneo (now Sabah) established a plant near Sandakan for production of alcohol-based motor car fuel from Nipa sap. Both the plant and Sandakan motor vehicles operated successfully for two years, but high production costs forced the closure of the scheme.

Another distinctive palm of the coastal zone is the Nibong which, with its 20-metre (60-feet) tall trunks armed with masses of hard black spines, is very different in appearance from the Nipa. The trunk, hard and resistant to both marine wood-boring grubs and termites, is a valuable material, still used to make large marine fish traps and, split lengthwise into long strips, flooring in the houses of coastal communities.

Swamp Forests

Where large rivers meander through floodplains before emerging into the mangrove zone, there may be extensive areas of flat, low-lying, alluvial land, some of it below the level of the main riverbank, periodically flooded or waterlogged by fresh water. The fertility of this land is constantly maintained by the layers of rich sediment left behind by successive flooding and here freshwater swamp forests develop. Their appearance depends on frequency of flooding and degree of waterlogging. Usually, more waterlogging means shorter trees and nastier vegetation: spiny and knife-edged grass-like plants, such as *pandan*, abound in the wetter areas, ready to lacerate human intruders. In very low-lying areas, trees may not survive at all and instead there are permanent marshes with dense sedges and

open water. Where freshwater swamps can be drained or protected from damaging floods, they are very suitable for certain kinds of agriculture – including wet rice and oil palm – and, for this reason, there are few freshwater swamp forests left in Southeast Asia, many of the remainder occurring in eastern Borneo.

This habitat is generally poor in plant species but, in combination with adjacent dry land forest, supports some of the richest populations of large animal species in Borneo, including all the monkeys and apes, all the hornbills and, in the north-east of the island, elephants. No naturalist can afford to miss the almost certain sightings of wildlife that freshwater swamp forests have to offer, and a tour by boat on the lower Kinabatangan River in eastern Sabah will provide the best opportunities.

Peat swamp forests are very different from freshwater swamp forests. In Borneo, especially in western regions, they evolve when the mangrove forest zone moves seawards, perhaps when sea levels fall or where great loads of sediment are deposited offshore by rivers flowing from steep, rainy mountain ranges. As the mangrove zone shifts, it leaves behind areas of salty, sulphur-rich, acidic mud which sustain virtually no form of life. Any plants which do colonize this inhospitable zone eventually die and accumulate without rotting. As the depth of the dead vegetation increases, conditions change so that different arrays of plant species take over. Floodwaters with their rich input of sediments do not reach the peat swamps, so the soil is very infertile yet, perhaps surprisingly, it supports good stands of commercial timber, and many peat swamp forests have been heavily disturbed over the years. There are no easily accessible areas of protected peat forests in Borneo, but rainforest enthusiasts may find examples in western Brunei, at Loagan Bunut in Sarawak, at Sentarum Lake and near Mandor in West Kalimantan, and at Tanjung Puting in Central Kalimantan.

Riverine Forests and Lakes

Bornean riverbanks are lined with trees except where the soil has been newly formed by deposition of sediment, and where people have cultivated or settled. In the lowlands, where large rivers slowly but

continuously change course, there is typically a zone of fertile alluvial soil extending for some distance from the river's edge. As long as flooding is infrequent and the soil is not waterlogged, this zone is suitable for growth of many kinds of useful trees. Sometimes, congregations of fruit trees can be seen growing along the riverbanks, many of them massive and old, particularly durians and mangoes of various species. Even if no people live there now, such sites would have supported villages many years ago.

Lowland riverine forest which has not been settled is poor in tree species but excellent for viewing wildlife. Birds likely to be seen include egrets, kingfishers, hornbills, birds of prey and the Oriental Darter, also known as the Snakebird, a fish-eater closely resembling the cormorants, which pursues its prey under water, striking out with its sinuous neck and stabbing with its long beak. The mammal especially worth watching for is the unique Proboscis Monkey, which occurs only in Borneo and is almost entirely confined to certain riverine and mangrove forests. The male of this distinctive species is characterized by his huge pendulous nose – the female can boast only a small snub. Lowland rivers in many parts of Borneo contain crocodiles, while in the lower Mahakam River, East Kalimantan, there is an endangered form of freshwater dolphin, the Snubfin.

Inland, upriver from the floodplain, riverbanks gradually become more rocky and steep, and a different array of tree species lines the banks. Particularly beautiful are the Ensurai trees, large and darkly coloured, with oblong leaves, which overhang the middle reaches of some rivers and typically support clusters of many epiphytic plants on their branches.

Unlike an increasing number of rivers on mainland Asia, whose banks have been largely deforested, and whose waters have become drains for towns, industries and agricultural plantations, most Bornean rivers remain in good condition. With a few small exceptions, the only significant pollutant in Bornean rivers is sediment resulting from soil erosion. This river-borne sediment is partly due to natural erosion processes, but concentrations have increased in recent years as a result of logging activities and conversion of forest to alternative land use. Available evidence indicates that populations of freshwater fishes are still healthy and productive in most Bornean rivers.

Like lowland rivers, Borneo's natural freshwater lakes have long attracted human interest. Yet the intensity of use has always been slight and it is only now that some of these lakes are coming under pressure from logging, conversion of forest to plantations and new settlements in surrounding land. Lakes which are quite accessible to the visitor to Borneo include the Jempang-Melintang-Semayang complex off the lower Mahakam River in East Kalimantan and the oxbow lakes off the lower Kinabatangan River in Sabah. Both areas are of historical interest. The lower Mahakam River was the site of Borneo's earliest known kingdom, the Hindu kingdom of Mulawarman, and remained one of the main centres of power and trade on Borneo's east coast until the 19th century. The Kinabatangan is the earliest known focus of Chinese contact in eastern Borneo and likewise remained a significant centre of trade in forest products until the 19th century. These lakes are also excellent territory for wildlife enthusiasts, with chances to see such rarities as Hairy-nosed Otter, Flat-headed Cat (a nocturnal fish-eating specialist), Oriental Darter and Storm's Stork. The lower Mahakam region is of cultural interest, too, with a mix of various people and customs. There are also fine lake habitats at Loagan Bunut in Sarawak, Tasek Merimbun in Brunei, and Sentarum and Sumpa off the upper Kapuas River in West Kalimantan. The freshwater fisheries of the Bornean lakes are productive and, in some cases, of great significance to local human communities.

Dipterocarp Forests

These are the forests which once covered most of Borneo and which even now, despite clearance, logging and fire, are the most widespread. They occur in most natural, well-drained situations from just above sea level to an altitude of about 1,000 metres (3,300 feet). The upper limit varies from place to place, being lower on small mountains near the coast, and higher on large mountains like Kinabalu.

Dipterocarp forests have local variations but all of them have one feature in common: the majority of the large trees belong to a single plant family, the Dipterocarpaceae. There are over 270 species of dipterocarps in Borneo, many of which exceed 45 metres (150 feet) in height when mature and they supply the majority of the timber which comes out of Borneo. Their fruits, consisting of a rather hard, oily seed, in most species bearing two or more wings, appear only rarely, on average once or twice in each decade, but when fruiting does occur it is simultaneous among most of the dipterocarps in any one area and, typically, also among many other trees in the forest. At such times, the forest seems full of fruits in all manner of shapes and sizes, in the trees and carpeting the ground. In fact, even in the most abundant years less than 10 per cent of all trees bear fruits.

Truly lowland dipterocarp forests, on gently sloping terrain below 150 metres (500 feet) altitude, often contain relatively high densities of trees of the legume family, as well as massive strangling fig plants. These forests, before the extensive clearance of recent decades, once supported an abundance of large mammals and birds. There are no extensive tracts of undisturbed lowland dipterocarp forests left, but fine examples of this habitat can be seen in several protected areas including Gunung Palung Nature Reserve (West Kalimantan), Kutai National Park (East Kalimantan), Niah National Park (Sarawak) and Danum Valley Conservation Area (Sabah).

In some lowland dipterocarp forests, one of the most common tree species is a member of the laurel family. This is the Borneo ironwood or Belian, the wood of which is exceptionally dense and durable, lasting for many decades under humid tropical conditions without any form of treatment. This makes it much in demand for building bridges, fence posts, roof tiles and the support pillars for traditional houses. One of the most accessible ironwood forests is in Sepilok Forest Reserve in eastern Sabah. It is a humbling experience to know that the first little footbridge that one comes across if walking from the reserve entrance along the trail to the mangrove, is the slowly decaying trunk of an ironwood tree, which probably started life as a seed before the first European set foot in Borneo.

Low but rugged or steeply sloping hills within the lowland regions of Borneo often have a distinctive dipterocarp forest cover, with numerous but rather small trees, patchy ground cover and sparse animal life. Some of these hilly forests, like Lambir Hills National Park in Sarawak, are botanically very rich. Other dipterocarp forests – especially where there are coarse, sandy soils on moderate slopes – contain large numbers of aromatic Kapur trees, which were once exploited as a source of camphor.

At altitudes of 150-600 metres (500-2,000 feet), the dipterocarp forests in some parts of Borneo contain a greater diversity of plant life than the extreme lowlands, plus good stands of massive timber trees and a variety of wild fruit trees. On fine, sunny mornings after a rainy spell, in regions where there are not too many traditional hunting communities, these forests peal with the magical calls of gibbons, Argus Pheasants and hornbills.

From about 500 metres (1,600 feet) to the upper limit of dipterocarp forests, there is a chance of finding one of several species of the remarkable parasitic *Rafflesia* plant, which produces the largest flower in the world. A flower is either female or male. Appearing initially as a small bud, it slowly swells until the enormous reddish or orange flower, sometimes measuring nearly a metre (3 feet) across, bursts open. Its faint unpleasant smell attracts insects to act as pollinators. The flower lives only a matter of days before it begins to degenerate, the female eventually turning into a strange, blackish bun-like fruit full of tiny seeds. The *Rafflesia* has no stem or leaves, and survives by extracting nutrients from the root or stem of its host plant, a woody climbing species related to the cultivated grape. There is a fair possibility of being able to see *Rafflesia* flowers in the Rafflesia Virgin Jungle Reserve or around the south-eastern fringes of Kinabalu Park (Sabah) and at Gunung Gading National Park (Sarawak).

With increasing altitude, the land typically becomes steeper and more rocky, with razor-like ridge tops, and the forest changes in subtle ways. There are fewer and different sounds, as some lowland bird and insect species drop out from the animal community and mountain forms start to appear. Far from settlements, the human visitor keeps to ridge-top trails where possible and occasionally experiences momentary apprehension as strong breezes and rain clouds pass over, producing a ghostly silence as all animal life is stilled.

Heath Forests

Some parts of Borneo are particularly infertile, consisting of pure white sand or pale, silica-rich soils on flat or gently sloping terrain, where heavy rain over long periods has leached out virtually all the nutrients. The visible surface usually consists of a thin layer of blackish, slowly decaying plant material. The short forest which develops naturally on these so-called 'podzol' soils is known as heath forest or, locally, as *kerangas*, an Iban term which refers to areas which cannot grow rice. Often, about a metre (3 feet) below the surface of the ground, there is an iron-rich hard layer. During heavy rain, water cannot drain freely through this layer, and the soil above becomes waterlogged. During dry spells, however, the top layer of the ground may become very dry indeed, making heath forests susceptible to fire.

Heath forests contain many closely spaced small trees with thick leaves, often reddish-tinged, and various curious plants that have relationships with insects, in some cases lethal to the insects, in some cases co-operative. Usually, there are pitcher plants, along with various epiphytes that form mutually beneficial relationships with ants. For example, *Dischidia* has very thick leaves which coat tree branches and act to shelter colonies of ants, while *Myrmecodia* harbours ants in its thickened stem. The ants in turn provide the plants with scarce nutrients, in the form of the remains of dead insects and other food that they bring in.

Heath forests often occur near the coast but due to chance factors in geological history, flat areas of suitable parent rock may yield such conditions anywhere in Borneo. Heath forests occur, for example, at over 900 metres (3,000 feet) above sea level in the Maliau Basin of central Sabah and on the Usun Apau Plateau in Sarawak.

On the coastal plains of western and southern Borneo, an array of heath-like forest types has developed on soils which combine peat and podzolic elements. The stature of these *kerapah* forests, as they have been called, varies greatly from place to place, but typically is much higher than that of heath forests. Unlike heath forests, some *kerapah* forests contain commercially valuable timber trees. One of these trees, Jelutong Paya, was tapped for its latex, used in the manufacture of chewing gum, in the early years of this century. Another native plant of these forests is the red-stemmed Sealing-wax Palm, now a popular ornamental in Bornean towns.

Ultrabasic Forests

Scattered within an arc from northern to south-eastern Sabah are a series of outcrops and mountains of ultrabasic rock, several exceeding 1,200 metres (3,900 feet) in height, all protruding from beneath the sedimentary layers that constitute the bulk of the island of Borneo. Ultrabasic rock is unusual in that it contains relatively low concentrations of the mineral silica, the basic constituent of most rocks, and high concentrations of metals such as iron, manganese, chromium and nickel. The vegetation on ultrabasic soils varies greatly but is always different from that on other soils nearby. Ultrabasic forest is lower, with an even, closely spaced canopy in comparison to adjacent dipterocarp forest, for example, and generally this forest has rattans but few woody climbing plants. Some plant species, including rare orchids, seem to occur only in ultrabasic areas. There is an ultrabasic zone on Gunung Kinabalu, and other examples may be seen near Ranau, Telupid and at Silam near Lahad Datu in Sabah.

Limestone Habitats

Limestone outcrops occur in several regions of Borneo. There are extensive areas in the Sangkulirang Peninsula of East Kalimantan, but they remain unexplored. Some of the most spectacular limestone features in the world – including caves, passages and pinnacles – are found in Gunung Mulu National Park in Sarawak. Accessible limestone caves with visitor facilities can also be found at Niah in Sarawak and at Gomantong and Batu Punggul in Sabah. Many of the Bornean caves were inhabited by prehistoric people and some have proven to be among the key archaeological sites on the island, yielding tools, ornaments and burial artefacts dating back many thousands of years. Remains of coffins, several hundreds of years old, can be seen in several of the limestone caves near the lower Kinabatangan River in Sabah.

Almost all the Bornean limestone caves contain the roosting sites of bats and small birds known as swiftlets, some species of which produce edible nests. Outside the caves, limestone forms the basis for unusual plant communities containing many rare species, some of them attractive ornamental herbs such as *Begonia*.

Mountain Forests

In Borneo, forests extend well above the upper limit of the dipterocarp zone, to more than 3,300 metres (11,000 feet) on Gunung Kinabalu. The kinds of plants present change with altitude. There are no very large trees and few climbing plants and, in general, the higher the altitude, the lower is the overall tree canopy. The array of animal species is different from that in the dipterocarp forests. For example, various squirrels, treeshrews and rats are confined to mountain forests. But it is among the birds that differences from the lowland fauna are most apparent. Prominent mountain birds include the noisy, exuberant laughing-thrushes, which scour the forest in groups, and the greyish, orange-tinged Treepie, with its strange, harsh, bell-like call. At higher elevations, where the tree canopy is lowest, small birds such as warblers can be approached very closely. The forest also becomes quieter with increasing altitude, as there are progressively fewer animals, especially insects. The zone where dipterocarp forest gives way to mountain forest often contains many coniferous trees (relatives of the pines). It is here, in some regions, that one of Borneo's most spectacular yet elusive birds, Bulwer's Pheasant, makes its home.

As the dipterocarps disappear with increasing altitude, the forest becomes dominated by trees of the oak and laurel families. Attractive plants which are rare or absent in the lowlands, such as rhododendrons and pitcher plants, become evident. Eventually, these, too, disappear and the forest turns into moss-draped bushes.

Only about 7 per cent of Borneo is covered in mountain forests, but they are disproportionately important in the ecology of the island as a whole. For example, mountains generally receive much more rainfall than

lowlands, and the thick, cool vegetation 'strips' water from passing clouds, storing it in moss and other epiphytes, and functioning as a regulator of water supplies. Mountain forests also contain many rare and localized wild species. In the long term, as large tracts of lowland forests disappear, mountain forests will form a higher proportion of Borneo's total tree cover.

Habitats at Risk

Places free of human impact are becoming scarcer by the year in Borneo. As a general rule, any vegetation or habitat near to a road is unlikely to be entirely natural except in specific areas reserved for conservation. On closer inspection, roadside trees often turn out to be the edges of orchards, or plantations (such as rubber) or merely woody weeds. Around Kota Kinabalu, for example, much of the roadside tree cover consists of three species of very hardy, self-propagating *Acacia* introduced from the Australasian region. Even away from roads, some landscapes have been transformed drastically through farming and fires. Where there is repeated fire, almost all trees are eventually wiped out leaving an open landscape of coarse, extremely hardy *lallang* grass. By this stage, the land is usually reckoned to be useless and is abandoned, although in the past decade or so, *lallang* grassland has been used for commercial planting of hardy tree species in several regions of Borneo. In South Kalimantan, farmers have shown that it is also possible, by ploughing with cattle, to manage such degraded grassland for growing hill rice.

Until recently, secondary and logged forests have not attracted much attention except among local communities who have some direct interest in specific areas. During the past decade or so, however, biologists have found that these forests often contain a lot of wildlife. With a growing awareness, too, that most of Borneo's forests will eventually be secondary or logged, conservation biologists are now taking a bigger interest in exploring and identifying those areas which might, if allowed to regenerate, represent important

biodiversity conservation areas.

Good examples of protected secondary forests can be found in Batang Ai National Park in Sarawak and in the Kayan-Mentarang Nature Reserve in East Kalimantan. Forests that have been logged fairly recently and intensively can be seen along the route into Danum Valley, as well as in Tabin Wildlife Reserve in Sabah. At a glance, Sepilok Forest Reserve in Sabah appears to be undisturbed old growth forest. In fact, most of the dipterocarp forest on flat land in this reserve was logged by hand methods in the early decades of this century and subjected to foresters' silvicultural treatments, including poisoning of non-commercial trees.

In view of the many misleading statements that have been made in recent years about tropical deforestation, it is worth emphasizing here that extraction of timber is not the usual cause of deforestation in Borneo. Instead, deforestation is due to conversion of forests to plantations, or clearance with the aim of farming or staking a claim to land, or uncontrolled fire.

BORNEO'S ANIMAL DIVERSITY

Borneo has no wildlife spectacles such as great herds of large, easily seen animals. Instead, it has one of the richest diversities of animal life on earth, intimately linked in a complex web of relationships with the diversity of plants. Anyone in search of Bornean animals will need to spend time sharing their habitats, absorbing the atmosphere, learning to look and listen. But every effort will be repaid with a deeper understanding of this extraordinary world and the excitement of realizing just how much there is to be observed in every corner of the forest.

Mammals and Reptiles

The array of Bornean mammals is impressive. Perhaps the best known is the Orang-utan, whose name is derived from the Malay for 'forest person'. The Orang-utans which can be readily seen at 'rehabilitation centres' in the forests at Sepilok (Sabah), Semengoh (Sarawak) and Tanjung Puting (Central Kalimantan) are mostly immature individuals. Mature wild male Orang-utans, some of which wander over vast distances in the rugged interior of Borneo far from the

main breeding populations, have immense strength. They present a fearsome appearance yet there are no reliable records of them attacking humans. The calls of such males – long, resonant groans which are often uttered in the middle of quiet nights – are a special feature of the Bornean forests.

Other primates include the graceful and athletic gibbons, which are more likely to be heard before they are seen as their enchanting songs fill the forest at dawn, the long-tailed, pot-bellied leaf monkeys that crash noisily through the tree canopy, the Proboscis Monkey which makes its home in the swamps and floodplains, and the adaptable omnivorous macaques, which often raid gardens and plantations for food.

As well as monkeys, the trees abound with all manner of small creatures that scramble, climb and even 'fly'. Among them is the tiny Bornean Tarsier, active only at night, which has huge goggle eyes, delicate grasping hands and a long, straw-like tail. The Colugo or Flying Lemur is another nocturnal mammal which, though less active than some of its tree-dwelling neighbours, can glide considerable distances by using the furry membrane that extends from its hands to the tip of its tail.

Of Borneo's cat species, the largest is the rare Clouded Leopard. Its canine teeth and attractively patterned pelt were once favoured as body decorations by Bornean warriors. Smaller felines include the Leopard Cat and the fish-eating Flat-headed Cat which haunts the banks of lowland rivers.

The largest land mammal of all is the Asian Elephant, which is confined to lowlands and valleys in the extreme north-east of the island. Previously assumed to have been introduced to Borneo by one of the early sultans, it may be that the elephant is native. In either case, being concentrated in an area of rapid agricultural development, the elephant must now be rated as one of Borneo's endangered species. The rarest Bornean mammal is the Asian Two-horned Rhinoceros (often known as the Sumatran Rhinoceros), a diminutive relative of massive woolly rhinos which inhabited the forests of Europe and North America millions of years ago.

The most numerous mammals are bats, of which over 90 species are known in Borneo. This group includes the smallest mammals, some weighing just a few grams, as well as

---

Opposite: *Murut women cross a suspension bridge at Sapulut, Sabah.*

the large Flying Fox, which ranges over great distances to feed on nectar and fruits.

Another wide-ranging species is the Bearded Pig which, in remaining regions of extensive forest cover, occasionally forms massive groupings that move up and down mountain ranges in search of fallen fruits. The meat and fat of these pigs are traditionally important food items for people of interior Borneo.

There are some 160 species of snakes in Borneo, of which only a small minority – such as the cobras and the tiny but deadly krait – are poisonous, and human snakebite fatalities are extremely rare. Pythons can reach up to 6 metres (20 feet) in length but their main prey is wild pig and they are highly unlikely to pose a threat to humans. Most forest snakes are not only harmless but extremely shy and only too ready to slide out of sight at the first hint of a footfall.

Other than snakes, Borneo's reptiles include tortoises, freshwater terrapins, sea turtles, crocodiles and many species of lizards, ranging from slender gliding lizards to the Water Monitor which reaches a length of over 2 metres (nearly 8 feet). There are nearly one hundred species of frogs, each preferring a slightly different habitat.

Birds

Birdlovers find plenty to interest them wherever they go in Borneo, as birds are the most noticeable and often the most spectacular of all the island's wildlife. Undisturbed forests anywhere in the lowlands and hills typically support about 200 resident species, and a day spent roaming with binoculars and notebook will satisfy the most ardent ornithologist. Logged forests are almost as rich a habitat but, although visibility is often better here, some sensitive species decline in numbers.

Every layer of the forest has its own inhabitants, from the pheasants and pittas skulking on the forest floor to the many species that frequent the high leafy canopy. Though not all are easy to spot at first glance, they are usually readily identified and located by their calls and songs. The majestic hornbills, revered in tribal folklore, are probably the most exciting – and impossible to miss – with their striking plumage, massive beaks often carrying a large horny casque, and loud swishing wing-

beats. Others include the woodpeckers, typical of their family in their noisy chatter and undulating flight, and the broadbills, recognizable by their bright colours and, as their name indicates, their heavy flattened beaks. With luck, and patience, a rare Bornean Bristlehead, its head topped by a spiky orange cap, may be sighted.

Mountain forests, secondary forests, coasts, wetlands and gardens each contain a different array of species. In coastal forests, the Long-tailed Parakeet (largest of Borneo's four members of the parrot family) and various attractive pigeons may be encountered. Egrets and herons grace wetlands throughout Borneo. Now common everywhere, sparrows were introduced into the island in 1964, but more interesting to see among garden birds are sunbirds, which feed on nectar and insects, the tailorbirds, which make nests by 'stitching' leaves together with fibres, and the melodious Magpie-robin. Mature oil palm, cocoa and abandoned rubber plantations near to forests also often support a surprising variety of species.

Insects

Most Bornean animals are insects and fortunately for the human traveller they are generally a friendly lot, there being only a few species of stinging bees and wasps. The butterflies form a prominent group, the most famous of which is undoubtedly the fabulous Rajah Brooke's Birdwing. Forest edges are often the best situations in which to seek butterflies. However, these insects are seasonal in occurrence and there is no guarantee of seeing any one species at any particular place or time. A place which can be recommended for observing butterflies year-round, however, is the hot springs area at Poring, Sabah, where many attractive species congregate in the flower-filled park.

Possibly the greatest diversity of insects occurs in the dipterocarp forests. Termites, for example, are represented by over one hundred species. These small insects superficially resemble ants both in form and in their habit of living in colonies of many thousands under, on and above the forest floor, but differ in their ability to burrow into and, in many cases, digest wood. Heard constantly in the dipterocarp forests but rarely seen are the cicadas, large

winged insects whose droning noises are produced by the vibration of membranes in cavities in the sides of their bodies.

Other major insect groups in Bornean forests include ants, beetles, bugs, moths, flies and thrips – the latter being important pollinators of many trees. There is no doubt that vast numbers of insect species remain to be discovered and described. Recent studies at Poring indicate that as many as a thousand species may live in just a single tree.

Marine Life

The warm seas around Borneo contain a dazzling array of fish in rainbow hues, as well as squid, jellyfish, dolphins, whales and turtles. Some are wide-ranging seasonal visitors. Dugongs – marine mammals which feed on sea grasses – occur but are extremely rare. These bulky seal-like creatures, though now protected by law, have suffered much from centuries of hunting.

Coral reefs, mainly off northern and north-eastern Borneo, have attracted much interest recently, particularly with the current popularity of scuba diving. Coral growth varies according to the movement of the seas. Where the currents are strongest, growth tends to be low and stoutly constructed but in deeper, calmer water the corals can branch out in a myriad delicate shapes. Corals alone form a diverse and spectacular group of organisms, but they also form the basis of a complex underwater ecological web which involves fishes and a colourful world of sea anemones, sea urchins, sea stars, sea slugs and many others.

The locations at which coral reefs can form are limited by depth of the sea bed and by water quality; they will not be found near the mouths of the large silt-laden rivers of Borneo. Some coral reefs are now threatened by localized increases in turbidity of marine waters or by illegal bombing by transient fishermen. But there are several coral-rich sites, such as Sipadan, off Sabah, and those at the Maratua group of islands of East Kalimantan, which remain in very good condition, and here divers can revel in the stunning abundance and beauty of an underwater paradise. Other sites – including the island parks and the lovely Semporna islands off Sabah – now enjoy increased protection so that, with time, they have a good chance to recover their original glory.

HISTORY AND GOVERNMENT

Until three decades ago, Borneo was covered mainly in a blanket of unbroken tropical rainforest, which to many outsiders gave the false impression that, for most of its history, the island had remained the domain of a thin scattering of forest peoples. However, along with discoveries of artefacts in several parts of Borneo, local legends indicate that the pattern of distribution of the people of interior Borneo has changed constantly. Some remote forests show evidence in their form and composition that certain areas of land were probably cultivated hundreds of years ago. Ancient imported artefacts and Chinese records suggest that there has been a continual flow of contacts with traders and settlers from other lands for at least the past one and a half millennia.

European influence on Borneo is relatively recent and is seen today primarily in the way in which the island is divided between three nations. From early historical times, trade was a key factor in influencing how and where native people lived. It was the Chinese, rather than the Europeans, who influenced the quantity and use of forest products collected by Bornean natives up to the late 19th century. Even into the early decades of the 20th century, Chinese trading junks continued to visit Borneo in large numbers every year. Whereas the Europeans arrived in search of gold, diamonds, pepper and regional strategic bases, the Chinese continued to trade in the whole range of forest and marine produce that they had been obtaining for centuries previously.

PREHISTORIC PEOPLES

The earliest people in South-east Asia were closely related to modern humans but of a different species. Fossil remains of the so-called Java Man, *Homo erectus*, more than one million years old, are known from the island of Java and it is likely that Java Man lived in Borneo too. Evidence of the oldest humans, *Homo sapiens*, in Borneo is provided by a skull excavated in the Niah caves of northern Sarawak, where the surrounding charcoal has been dated at about 40,000 years old.

In the limestone outcrops of Madai and Baturong in Sabah there is further evidence of human settlement dating back about 30,000 years. Around this period a lava flow caused by volcanic activity blocked off a river in the vicinity of the Baturong outcrop, forming a large lake. For several thousands of years, until the river broke through allowing water to drain away, Baturong was situated at the centre of the lake. Stone tools have been found at what was once the water's edge, and discoveries of shells and bones show that the lakeside dwellers fed on large quantities of freshwater molluscs and forest animals. Around 9,000 years ago, the centre of human activity shifted to the Madai caves, much nearer to the coast than Baturong, and these people lived on shellfish from nearby mangroves as well as a variety of forest animals. About 7,000 years ago, the caves were abandoned until a new human society started making use of them again 4,000 years later. By this time, people had the ability to cultivate plant crops and to make pottery.

The people indigenous to Borneo tens of thousands of years ago appear to have been replaced by a race of migrants from mainland Asia, known to anthropologists as Austronesians. The name is rather confusing, as these people are the ancestors of the present-day natives of Borneo, and the Austronesians have nothing to do with Australia. The exact timing and means of arrival of these Austronesians is unknown. A common belief is that they originated from southern China, moving through Taiwan, and reaching Borneo on outrigger canoes via the Philippine Islands some time after 4,000 BC. The Austronesians brought with them a variety of concepts and items which set in motion massive changes in the lifestyle of the earlier hunter-gatherers. Among these were cultivated cereal crops (notably rice), sugar-cane, pigs (for eating), dogs (for hunting), pottery, weaving and improved methods of making tools and weapons.

The picture of development of human societies and technologies in Borneo from around 3,000 to 1,000 years ago is still unclear. There are numerous indications from archaeological finds within the South-east Asian region, however, that it was during this period that many of the key elements of modern societies evolved. From Niah alone, there are various kinds of polished stone tools, shell and bone ornaments, and remains of *pandan* mats, bamboo caskets and wooden coffins, some dating back more than 2,000 years. Some activities, such as the cultivation of various food crops, must have been developed by indigenous farmers in Borneo during this period, but important new ideas and materials were probably being brought into the island by traders and new settlers.

The first use of metals – copper and bronze – by people in the South-east Asian region seems to have begun some time before 500 BC in southern Vietnam and northern Thailand. The earliest copper implements so far discovered in Borneo, dating back 2,000 to 2,500 years, come from the Tapadong and Madai caves in Sabah. Iron spear-heads and polished stone tools have been found at similar depths in the same caves. It would seem that, in Borneo, there was no sharp separation in time in the use of stone, copper and iron tools. Yet the introduction of metal tools would have revolutionized life for people living in a zone which is naturally covered in tropical rainforest. The ability to clear forest for crops which require open land, especially rice, would have been made very much easier than before, once sharp axes and long knives suitable for hacking were available.

It was possibly not until after AD 500, however, that iron was both mined and fashioned for use within Borneo. Availability of metals had another important implication. Long, iron boring tools are needed to permit ironwood poles to be converted into blowpipes, the best type of weapon for hunting tree-dwelling food items such as hornbills and monkeys.

There are several regions with iron ore deposits in Borneo. Major areas include the Apo Kayan (East Kalimantan), upper Barito (Central Kalimantan), Sambas and Tayan off the Kapuas River (West Kalimantan) and the Sarawak River. There seems to be some relationship between these concentrations of iron ore and the oddly scattered distribution of the main groups of inland people of Borneo. Another factor which probably had a bearing on the early distribution of people in the interior of Borneo was the occurrence of salt.

EARLY HISTORICAL INFLUENCES

The earliest contacts with people from outside the region immediately surrounding Borneo seem to have been with India. It is not clear if Indians had direct contact with Borneo, or whether the influence was via Indian settlements elsewhere, especially in Java and Sumatra. Artefacts with clear Hindu Indian influence, believed to date from the 4th century AD, have been found along the Mahakam River of East Kalimantan. At that time, the kingdom of Martapura was ruled by King Mulawarman from the junction of the Kedang Kepala tributary with the Mahakam River. There are also Hindu ruins and statues possibly dating from this early period around the Barito River in South Kalimantan and near Sambas in West Kalimantan. Ornaments, inscriptions and statues of Indian origin or influence, believed to date from the 6th or 7th century AD, have been found at Limbang in northern Sarawak.

There is a surprising connection between southern Borneo and Madagascar, 5,000 kilometres (3,000 miles) away on the other side of the Indian Ocean. The languages of both areas contain common words, including some derived from the ancient Sanskrit language of India. It is believed that the similarity in language dates back to a migration of south Bornean people to Madagascar some time after AD 400.

THE CHINESE CONNECTION

Over the past one and a half thousand years, connections between Borneo and China have occurred more frequently than those with India, as Chinese artefacts found in Borneo and old Chinese texts on trade with the region bear evidence. Unfortunately, the old texts give place names which have changed with the passage of time and their locations cannot be traced with certainty. Chinese Buddhist pilgrims journeyed to India starting in the 3rd and 4th centuries, and it is likely that they would have stopped off on the west coast of Borneo for water and food. One of the earliest definite links is the presence of Chinese ceramics and coins at Terusan Kupang, 5 kilometres (3 miles) upriver from Bandar Seri Begawan in Brunei, which were found in deposits dated at around AD 750.

The name of Po-ni, from which both Brunei and Borneo are believed to derive, is mentioned repeatedly in Chinese texts starting from the 9th century AD. The balance of opinion is that Po-ni was on the west side of Borneo, probably within Brunei Bay, and possibly at the mouth of the Lawas River. Other ancient Chinese names which appear to refer to Borneo include Po-lo, Po-li and Y-po-ti. Tribute missions were sent occasionally from Po-ni to China during early times, with specific records of these events for the years 631, 977, 1082 and 1405. Finds of Chinese porcelain, stoneware and coins at Santubong in Sarawak are believed to date mainly from the 10th century.

EARLY TRADE IN A WIDER PERSPECTIVE

The Chinese were not the only early traders with Borneo. An Arab sea captain wrote around the year AD 950 of a place called Sribuza, situated in a large bay on an island, believed to have been Borneo. In the *Book of Delights*, written by an Arab in 1154, a place named Muja, probably Borneo, was described as producing the world's best camphor.

Early traders coming to Borneo brought with them metal goods, pottery, beads and cloth, and a wide range of goods were obtained in return. Trade on the west coast of Borneo was influenced around AD 800 by the Sumatran-based Buddhist empire of Srivijaya. At that time, one of the centres of camphor export was Tawaran, believed to be present-day Tuaran just north of Kota Kinabalu in Sabah. By AD 1000, due to wars with Java, the Sumatrans had lost their power in Borneo. From then on Po-ni, or Brunei, itself developed into a small empire encompassing Sarawak, Sabah and the Philippines. Its major trading partner continued to be China.

In 1225, Chau Ju Kua, a controller of customs in China's Fukien Province, recorded that Po-ni was the most important port, with the most developed form of government, in the region now encompassing Indonesia, Malaysia and the Philippines. At this time, Po-ni boasted more than a hundred warships.

Around 1260, the Java-based Hindu empire of Majapahit began to expand, and by the 1300s the Majapahits had succeeded in dominating trade on western and southern Borneo. They used the name of Buruneng for their trading centre, presumed to be Brunei and the same place as Po-ni.

A Chinese record of 1349 mentions the fine quality of pearls from Sulu, off the north-east coast of Borneo and formerly under the control of the Brunei kingdom, which at that time was growing in strength. In 1369, a force from Sulu sacked Brunei. The Suluks were then driven out by a Majapahit rescue fleet, but the power of the Majapahits in Borneo declined during the 14th century.

THE COMING OF ISLAM

The time of the first Muslim contact with Borneo is uncertain. One Chinese scholar has suggested that the earliest gravestone of a Muslim sultan in Brunei dates from AD 1301, having been shipped from China. Other sources suggest that Islam has been spreading through Borneo since around the early 1400s when, coincidentally, at least two Muslims from different parts of the world visited what is now Sabah. One, an Arab missionary named Machdom, came to Sulu via Melaka (formerly spelled Malacca; on the west coast of the Malay Peninsula), building the first mosque on Pulau Simunul in 1380. An ancient document in Arabic *jawi* script, still retained by the Idahan people of Sapagaya on the fringe of Darvel Bay in eastern Sabah, indicates that Machdom visited Darvel Bay in 1408, converting the inhabitants to Islam.

Also sometime around 1400, at least one and possibly two Chinese fleets visited the Sulu and Brunei regions and, according to legend, made trips up the Kinabatangan River. Old Chinese texts report that a Muslim admiral named Cheng Ho visited Sulu with 60 vessels and travelled extensively in the region. The royal annals of Brunei record that a Muslim Chinese voyager, Ong Sum Ping, visited Brunei at this period, and that one of his female relatives married the second Muslim Sultan of Brunei. A legend from Sulu has it that a Chinese princess from a settlement on the Kinabatangan River married a ruler of Brunei. Precisely what events occurred will

Early photographs of some of Borneo's indigenous people.

Above: *Putatan Dusun women wearing brass ring girdles and belts made from silver dollars.*

Right: *A Murut chief. The Murut and Dusun are descendants of Sabah's earliest inhabitants.*

Far right: *Two Sea Dayaks, now known as Iban, in war dress. The Iban are Sarawak's largest group of inland farmers.*

never be known, but it seems likely that both Cheng Ho and Ong Sum Ping were members of the same fleet and that both were instrumental in spreading Islam in northern Borneo. It is also apparent that marriages between Chinese voyagers and Borneo natives occurred during this period.

In 1408, for the first time, the King of Po-ni himself visited China in a 150-strong group including his family, seemingly to reinforce Brunei's links with China and to seek to sweep away the diminishing power of both Majapahit and Sulu in northern Borneo. This king, Maharaja Karna, died a month after his arrival at the imperial capital of Nangking and was buried outside the town. The Emperor of China bade the group from Po-ni – minus their ruler – return to Borneo, and decreed that Po-ni should have a state mountain. He gave the group an inscribed stone to be set on top of the mountain, which was to be called the Mountain of Lasting Tranquillity Preserving the State. Thus, Po-ni became known to the Chinese as the Land of Lasting Tranquillity. This name was translated into the Arabic 'Darussalam' ('Abode of Peace').

It seems that during the 15th and 16th centuries, Islam spread through the coastal regions of Borneo. Also, links were established not only between native communities and China, but between coastal Bornean communities and other areas in South-east Asia. Brunei had links with Melaka, Sambas with Johor (in Peninsular Malaysia), while Banjarmasin had close relations with Java.

During the 16th century, Muslim dynasties were founded at Sambas, Sukadana and Landak on the west coast of Borneo and at Banjarmasin on the south coast. Like those of Brunei and Sulu, these coastal sultanates thrived by trading items from the interior and imposing taxes. To varying extents, the sultanates were also involved in piracy, sometimes raiding one another.

THE FIRST EUROPEAN CONTACTS

The first European visitor to Borneo was possibly an Italian, Ludovico de Varthema, who is reputed to have reached the island around 1505, but Portugal and Spain were the first European nations to take notice of Borneo as a centre of power and commerce. In 1511, Portugal captured Melaka

and made it their base for trade in Asia. The first description of Borneo from first-hand knowledge came from Tome Pires, supervisor of the Asian spice trade from 1512 to 1515, who recorded the arrival in Melaka of Bornean gold and camphor.

The earliest detailed description of Borneo by a visitor to the island is that of Antonio Pigafetta, the Italian chronicler of Magellan's Spanish fleet, which lost its leader during a skirmish with Cebu islanders in what is now the Philippines. Following Magellan's death, the remainder of his party sailed into Brunei Bay in July 1521 with only two of their original five ships afloat. Pigafetta, who wrote that Brunei town contained 25,000 families, found that the sultanate was the most impressive of the communities that Magellan's fleet visited on its pioneering journey.

From 1526, Brunei traded regularly with the Portuguese in Melaka and was a highly influential power in and around Borneo. The sultan of the period, referred to as Raja Sripada by Pigafetta, was probably Sultan Bolkiah, who exerted control over the sultans of Sambas, Sukadana and Banjarmasin. The Dutch captured Melaka in 1641, thus severing the Portuguese trading link with Brunei. The Portuguese established a new trading post on Borneo in 1690, at Martapura in the south, but withdrew after four years and thereafter made no fresh attempts to establish their presence on the island.

The Spanish government which had established itself in the northern Philippines made various attempts over the years to suppress Muslim influence – the Moros, as they were called – in the south. In the late 1570s, the Spanish sent expeditions to topple the Brunei sultan, but these failed. The activities of Brunei pirates led to another Spanish attack in 1645. Spain remained hostile to Borneo and never attempted to establish peaceful trade with the island.

EARLY DUTCH INFLUENCE

In 1600, the English East India Company was founded in order to develop trade in India and South-east Asia. Two years later, the Dutch East India Company was founded with the same objective. After the Spanish and Portuguese failed to show serious inter-

est in controlling Borneo trade, the Dutch were the next European power to move in, followed by the British. Initial Dutch interest was centred on the sultanate of Banjarmasin, with the aim of buying pepper. But the Dutch were to find that in Borneo simple objectives were not always simply implemented. In 1603, a trading post was opened at Banjarmasin, but the murder of some Dutch traders a few years later sparked off hostilities and in 1612 the Dutch destroyed the town, forcing the sultan to move to Martapura. A similar pattern of murder and revenge plagued Dutch enterprise in southern and western Borneo throughout the 17th century.

At the end of the century, the Dutch began to realize that the peaceful opening of trade would not achieve results. They started to use the techniques of aggression and the playing off of one native faction against another as the way to achieve control. In 1698, the Raja of Landak in western Borneo appealed to the Sultan of Bantam, on the island of Java, for help in fighting his neighbouring sultan at Sukadana. A combined Dutch-Bantam-Landak force wiped out Sukadana and the Javanese Sultan of Bantam became recognized as the supreme ruler of western Borneo. Although Bantam is a long way from western Borneo, its sultan was a vassal of the Netherlands, and so this action meant that the Dutch East India Company had rapidly acquired considerable authority over western Borneo.

In 1772, an Arab pirate and adventurer named Abdu'r-Rahman established himself at the then small village of Pontianak, near the mouth of the Landak River, without the permission of the Raja of Landak. The raja complained to the Sultan of Bantam, who had by that time completely surrendered his sovereign rights over western Borneo to the Dutch. The Dutch, however, decided not to support the raja but instead granted Abdu'r-Rahman recognition as 'Sultan of Pontianak'. They installed a trading post at Pontianak and encouraged the new sultan to suppress any state in the area which refused to accept his supremacy. Thus was established the sultanate of Pontianak and the demise of the other rulers of south-western Borneo.

The Dutch played a similar game in southern Borneo. The Dutch East India

Company had in 1747 negotiated yet another pepper contract with the Sultan of Banjarmasin, which this time included the establishment of a government fort. With the start of an invasion by the Bugis people and internal quarrelling in the sultanate in 1785, the Dutch were provided with the opportunity to interfere in support of their trading interests. They sided with one contestant for power, ensured that he won his battles, and installed him as sultan on condition that he cede his newly acquired dominion to the Netherlands Indian government. Thus, in 1787, the Dutch East India Company became 'the sovereign lord, owner, and possessor of the whole kingdom of Banjarmasin', the first foreign power to take full control of Bornean land.

Within a short period, however, the Dutch achievement of being the only significant European power in Borneo disintegrated. The 1784 Treaty of Paris had opened the South-east Asian archipelago to the ships of all nations, thus breaking the virtual monopoly of the Dutch in the East Indies. In any case, years of overspending, inadequate accounting and corruption had reduced the Dutch East India Company to the verge of bankruptcy. As part of their cost-saving attempts, the Dutch authorities in Java decided in 1790 that all Dutch settlements in western Borneo should be abandoned. Later, in 1797, the lands ceded by the Sultan of Banjarmasin in southern Borneo were handed back to him. The last of the early Dutch settlements in Borneo, Fort Tatas near Banjarmasin, was abandoned in 1809.

NORTHERN BORNEO AND THE BRITISH

Meanwhile, there were changes in northern Borneo. After Pigafetta's pioneering visit, internal power struggles grew commonplace in Brunei and the sultanate's power declined. In the middle of the 17th century, the chief minister of Brunei, Pengiran Bongsu, overthrew his sultan with the aid of the Sultan of Sulu. In return for this help, the Sultan of Sulu assumed control of the coastal zone between Kimanis Bay (now western Sabah) and the Sebuku River (now East Kalimantan).

In the wake of the Dutch, the English

East India Company had also taken an interest in Borneo, not so much for obtaining produce directly from the island, but as a base from which to expand its existing operations in Asia. Alexander Dalrymple, a Company employee in Madras, visited the Sulu archipelago several times between 1759 and 1764, and obtained from the Sultan of Sulu an agreement for the cession of territory in northern Borneo, including some offshore islands. Dalrymple chose Balambangan island as the location for the Company's trading station, apparently because he calculated that it was in the centre of an imaginary circle encompassing the East Indies. It was not until 1772 that troops, stores and trade goods were sent to Balambangan island by the English East India Company, by which time Dalrymple had been dismissed from the Company's service. Instead of Dalrymple, the Company sent John Herbert as chief of the new Balambangan trading centre. The major items of trade brought in by Herbert were guns, gunpowder and opium.

In 1773, the old sultan abdicated in favour of one of his sons. Relations with the undiplomatic Herbert deteriorated and in 1775 the settlement was attacked and destroyed by a Sulu force. The Company tried again to open trading posts on Balambangan and in Brunei in 1803, but both were closed down after a year. In 1812, on the orders of Thomas Stamford Raffles in Java, Captain John Hunt conducted detailed surveys of trade in Sulu and north-eastern Borneo. Hunt reported favourably on the region, but no action was taken.

THE VAGARIES OF HISTORY

The abandonment of Borneo by the Dutch was a potential disaster for the Sultan of Banjarmasin, as he was in no position to defend his once prestigious and powerful territory alone. He sought support from various authorities in the region but initially none was forthcoming.

From the late 18th century, a number of European venturers came to Borneo with various motives. One example was Alexander Hare, a British merchant based in Melaka. In 1810, Hare sent two trading vessels to Banjarmasin, which returned with absolutely nothing. In pursuit of his evident

desire to found a kingdom and acquire slaves and a harem, however, Hare decided that Borneo was a land of boundless opportunities. When the Sultan of Banjarmasin sent two envoys to Melaka in search of support for his declining power, Hare introduced them to the newly appointed 'Agent to the Governor-General with the Malay States', Stamford Raffles.

The timing was perfect for the aims of all parties. Following Napoleon's annexation of Holland in 1810, the British decided to invade Java, seat of Dutch power in the East Indies. Officially, Raffles was charged by the British government with the job of planning for the invasion, but such was his interest and vision that he took it upon himself to make contacts with the sultans of the entire region. Although he had not been to Borneo, he was convinced that it was 'not only one of the most fertile countries in the world, but the most productive in gold and diamonds'.

In 1812, Hare was sent to Banjarmasin, as 'British Resident' to found a settlement. A treaty was negotiated by Hare, which ceded to the English East India Company most of south-eastern Borneo with the exception of 3,600 square kilometres (1,400 square miles) granted by the sultan to Hare himself. In fact, the Sultan of Banjarmasin got the better end of the bargain, as he exerted almost no real control over the territory that he had ceded, but gained power in the eyes of local rivals.

Hare set about grand schemes to grow pepper and rice, mine diamonds, export forest produce and make salt. It soon became apparent, as it was to become apparent repeatedly with almost every development scheme throughout Borneo up to the present day, that the local native population was too small and was not happy to work as planned by developers from elsewhere. Upwards of 3,200 people were brought in from Java, mostly against their will, to work in Banjarmasin.

During the few years that it took to get these people to Banjarmasin, events had conspired to make the whole exercise unnecessary. Raffles, now Lieutenant-Governor of Java, had come to believe that the existing communities on western Borneo offered better trading prospects than Banjarmasin in the south-east. In any case, as the war against Napoleon drew to a close, the British government decided that, on balance, a strong Netherlands government would now be to their advantage. It was realized that this in turn would depend on the Dutch being supported by the prosperity of their overseas colonial possessions. It was on this basis that the apportionment of tropical colonies between Britain and the Netherlands was mutually agreed. It was decided that the bulk of the East Indies would be returned to the Dutch.

THE DUTCH CONSOLIDATION OF POWER IN THE SOUTH

The Netherlands was not particularly interested in Borneo, but the British were even less so. In 1816, first Hare and then Britain officially withdrew from Banjarmasin. In 1817, the Sultan of Banjarmasin signed yet another agreement, this time ceding all territory between Kota Waringin and Berau to the Dutch government, in return for which the Dutch would protect the sultan, his people and the land ceded against all native and foreign enemies. As in the case of the previous agreement, the sultan had only a tenuous claim over most of the land that he had ceded.

Following the lead, the Sultan of Sambas on western Borneo, a notorious pirate, wrote to the new Dutch government in Java, suggesting a similar arrangement. Soon afterwards, another letter expressing friendship was received in Java from his rival the Sultan of Pontianak. A Dutch force was sent to western Borneo in 1818 to negotiate treaties with both sultans and other leaders in the region. The idea was to gain customs revenues and promote peaceful trade in return for giving military support to the sultans when needed. The Dutch expedition went to Pontianak first and quickly made a deal. Proceeding to Sambas, the Dutch met the sultan himself at the mouth of the Sambas River, at the front of a fleet of warboats, just setting out for Pontianak on a pirate raid. The raid was cancelled, a treaty negotiated, and the Dutch had consolidated their power in west and south Borneo.

Not everyone on the British side was happy with Borneo being left to the Dutch. British traders in Penang were especially alarmed, while Stamford Raffles, now

Lieutenant-Governor of Bencoolen in Sumatra, felt that Britain should actively seize control of most of Borneo except Banjarmasin. The whole question of apportioning control of the various parts of the East Indies between the British and Dutch governments dragged on until the 1830s. Both sides were more preoccupied with areas other than Borneo, such as Melaka, Singapore and Sumatra, so neither side actively pursued acquisition of more areas in Borneo.

Within the East Indies, many Dutchmen wanted to extend their power northwards in Borneo, especially through the still powerful Sultan of Brunei. But the central government continually had more pressing issues to resolve. In 1823, a Dutch envoy had visited Brunei, but not concluded any treaty. In 1831, the government in Java sent a Sambas nobleman to negotiate on the Dutch behalf. He remained in Brunei for nine months, apparently enjoying a long holiday, and returned empty-handed.

In 1838-1839, the Dutch Assistant Resident in Sambas, R. Bloem, argued to his government that a treaty with the Sultan of Brunei was needed urgently in order to reduce smuggling and forestall British influence in western Borneo. His appeals fell on unsympathetic ears. In fact, the British government had no special interest in western Borneo at that time and, but for the coming of one British adventurer, Bloem's concern would have been excessive and the Dutch might have come to control all of Borneo.

THE BROOKES AND SARAWAK

In 1839, James Brooke, a former officer in the English East India Company army now seeking adventure, arrived in his ship, the *Royalist*, at the mouth of the Sarawak River. This event signalled a profound change in the way the pattern of developments in Borneo would subsequently unfold. The hundred-year rule of the 'White Rajahs' of Sarawak was soon to commence. In return for his services in helping to quell rebellion in its distant Sarawak River province, Brunei in 1841 ceded the land between Tanjung

James Brooke, first of the 'White Rajahs', and (below) *Ranee Margaret, Consort to the second Rajah, Charles Brooke, with attendant noblewomen.*

His Royal Highness, Sri Paduka Al Sultan Mohamet Jamal Al Alam bin Sri Paduka Al Marhom Al Sultan Mohamet Fathlon, Sultan of Sulu, with his royal entourage, c. 1876. The once-powerful sultanate, which during the preceding century had held sway over the trade and peoples of north-east Borneo, was now in decline. In July 1878 the sultan was forced to yield sovereignty of Sulu to the Spanish government of the Philippines. In the previous January, however, he had ceded most of what is now Sabah to Baron von Overbeck and Alfred Dent for an annual compensation of Straits $5,000.

Datu and the Samarahan River to Brooke, who assumed the title of 'rajah'. Through luck, charm, swashbuckling and sometimes bloodthirsty battles with real and purported pirates, helped out by the British navy, Brooke continued to consolidate his power and acquire more territory from Brunei.

James Brooke died in 1868 and was succeeded by his nephew Charles who, although taking a more peaceful and less colourful approach, extended the family's territory to Lawas, thereby drawing the boundary for the future Malaysian state of Sarawak. During the later years of James's reign, the existence and sometimes ruthless policies of the Brooke rule had aroused considerable contention in Britain, and it was not until 1888 that official British government protection for Sarawak was granted. Charles Brooke's son, Charles Vyner Brooke, took over in 1917. After a century of Brooke family rule, in 1941 Charles Vyner drafted a written constitution for Sarawak as a first step towards introducing more democracy, but soon afterwards the Japanese invaded.

PIRACY AND SLAVE-TRADING

Piracy and slave-trading had become rife around Borneo by the 19th century. Both activities were promoted by Malay nobles of all the coastal communities, including Brunei. Often, pirate raids were abetted by one nobleman as part of his plan to destabilize or cripple the power of another. Thus, there was a continual flux in who wielded power and where. In many cases, pirate leaders were men of Arab descent – known in the 19th century as *sherifs* – whose followers included Borneo natives, both Muslim and non-Muslim. Most feared by the coastal people of Borneo, however, were groups from what is now the southern Philippines. Especially dreaded were the Illanun, who often raided independently, and who used ships nearly 30 metres (100 feet) long powered by two decks of slave oarsmen. Their weapons included brass cannons. On long expeditions – sometimes lasting up to three years – whole Illanun communities including women and children would be carried on a third deck above the oarsmen. When not at sea, pirate bands were based in forts on the lower reaches of the rivers of northern and western Borneo. From the 1840s to the 1870s, the British navy successfully destroyed the major bands and forts at Saribas, Batang Lupar (Sarawak), Membakut, Tempasuk, Marudu and Tungku (Sabah).

BRITAIN AND 19TH-CENTURY NORTH BORNEO

The British government supported James Brooke in Sarawak but claimed no rights there. In 1846, the island of Labuan was ceded by the Sultan of Brunei to the British government, which appointed Brooke as Governor and Consul-General of this, the first territory of the British Empire in northern Borneo. Early hopes that Labuan would become a key trading centre like Singapore never materialized. Malaria, various conflicts within the British government, the inability of the island's coal mines to sell coal and the high cost of maintaining a strategically useless base led the British eventually in 1902 to make Labuan part of the Straits Settlements, administered along with Penang, Melaka and Singapore.

In the meantime, a series of strange events had set the course of history for the northern end of mainland Borneo. In 1865, an American named Lee Moses obtained a lease on land which is now Sabah from the Sultan of Brunei, later selling the lease to the American Trading Company, which failed to prosper. In 1875, Baron von Overbeck, an Austrian government officer stationed in Hong Kong, bought over the lease and joined with the Dent Brothers, British merchants in Hong Kong. Overbeck then learned from the governor of Labuan that Sabah had been given to the Sultan of Sulu by Brunei two centuries earlier. Assisted by Scotsman William Cowie, a trader who supplied guns to the Sultan of Sulu, Overbeck visited Sulu and obtained North Borneo for payment of Straits $5,000 annually. British officers were placed in the territory. Overbeck then sold his share to the Dents, who in 1881 successfully obtained a royal charter which gave the British North Borneo (Chartered) Company the right to rule North Borneo. Early hopes that gold, then tobacco, would bring prosperity came to nothing. The Company relied on taxes and customs duties to survive and rarely made profits.

COLONIALISM IN BORNEO

Brunei remained under British protection but was never a colony. The three European rulers of Borneo from the 19th century up to the Japanese invasion in 1941 differed in their approaches. To the Dutch, Borneo was a large but underpopulated part of their massive East Indies territory, difficult to develop yet important by the early 20th century as a source of petroleum. Christian missionaries were encouraged, starting as early as the 1830s, and the spread of Islam was suppressed. From the early 20th century, there were considerable attempts at developing an organized basic system of communications, medical facilities and education. After bloody clashes in James Brooke's earlier years, Sarawak was ruled as a benign autocracy from the 1860s, with virtually no pressure put on the indigenous people to change in any way, and a fair degree of freedom given to administering officers to use common sense in the area of their posting. Missionaries and foreign entrepreneurs – including British ones –

A police patrol on a bamboo raft at Maligan, in south-western Sabah, 1910.

were forbidden. Apart from the opening of oil fields at Miri, there was no attempt at promoting commerce.

The British North Borneo Company, not surprisingly, was the most commercially minded ruler. When expectations that North Borneo was rich in gold proved unfounded, agricultural plantations were encouraged through leasing of large land areas to British, Dutch and also Japanese plantation companies. In fact, only small areas were ever planted, mainly with tobacco and rubber. Although dwarfed by the huge trade of recent decades, tropical hardwood export was one of the features of North Borneo from its early days. Between the two World Wars, the Company actively encouraged Chinese immigrants.

There were many localized incidents of conflict and occasional attacks on European invaders by indigenous people during the period of colonial expansion. Borneo remained generally free of serious conflict, however, perhaps because there was never a large foreign population at any one time, no competition for land and little interference with native customs. Prior to 1941, the maximum number of Europeans on the island was less than 8,000, mostly concentrated in Dutch oil-producing enclaves on the east coast. Head-hunting was the only

indigenous custom that the Europeans consistently tried to eradicate. The most colourful and persistent rebel was Mat Salleh, a Suluk-Bajau, who began to challenge the rule of the Company in 1894 and was eventually killed by the British in 1900.

THE SECOND WORLD WAR AND INDEPENDENCE

The Japanese invasion of Borneo in December 1941 had a profound impact on the future of the island. Europeans were rounded up everywhere, even in the remotest interior, and many died, either on capture, or on the notorious Death March of prisoners of war between Sandakan and Ranau in Sabah. When the Japanese surrendered to Australian forces in September 1945, the main towns of North Borneo had been demolished by Allied bombing. European supremacy had been lost, both physically and in the minds of many Borneans. Many people of the former Dutch East Indies, especially in Java, refused to allow the Dutch to return, and Indonesia declared itself an independent nation in 1945. A combination of active resistance against the Dutch in Java and diplomatic efforts led eventually to international recognition of independence in 1949.

American adventurers Martin and Osa Johnson visited British North Borneo in the 1930s, using a seaplane. A posed photograph shows them on the Kinabatangan River.

Britain decided that North Borneo and Sarawak should be ceded to the Crown and a new treaty negotiated with the Sultan of Brunei. The people of North Borneo agreed but there was some resistance in Sarawak, including the assassination of the governor in 1949, before the majority agreed to British rule.

The Sultan of Brunei left to live in Kuching and after his death his brother took his place. Infrastructure was slowly but steadily built up in North Borneo and Sarawak during the 1950s, and air services linking these states with Singapore and Malaya were introduced.

The first Prime Minister of Malaya, Tunku Abdul Rahman, proposed in 1961 that the Borneo states might join Malaya to form an enlarged federation of Malaysia. There was a mixed reaction from the people of these states and opposition from Indonesia – the so-called 'Confrontation', which involved the stationing of British and Australian troops in Borneo and skirmishes at the border regions. Despite these tribulations, added to by a brief rebellion in Brunei, Sabah (North Borneo) and Sarawak achieved independence through Malaysia in

1963. Brunei chose to retain its status of British protectorate and achieved independence in 1984.

GOVERNMENT TODAY

The three nations represented in Borneo, although superimposed on similar environments, practise distinctly different forms of government.

Brunei

Brunei is a Malay Muslim monarchy, in which the position of the ruler, a sultan, is inherited. Under the Constitution of 1959, the sultan is advised by four Councils (Religious, Privy, Cabinet and Succession). There are no political organizations in Brunei. An important role of the sultan, who is also the Prime Minister and Defence Minister, is to maintain unity, nurturing Islam (the Muslim religion) and Brunei Malay culture. Several of the sultan's family members have roles in government, for instance as ministers of Finance and of Foreign Affairs. Brunei is divided into four administrative districts, each headed by a District Officer, who reports directly to the Prime Minister. The country's enormous wealth, derived from an oil- and petroleum-based economy, ensures that its people enjoy one of the highest standards of living in South-east Asia, with free medical care and education and, for many, secure employment in government and related services.

Malaysia

Sabah and Sarawak are two of the thirteen states of the Malaysian federation, which has a king, known as the Yang di-Pertuan Agong, appointed under a National Constitution. The king is elected by, and from among, hereditary Malay rulers in nine of the Peninsular Malaysian states, for a term of five years. Neither Sabah nor Sarawak has a hereditary Malay ruler, and instead each has a head of state appointed by the king. The powers of the king and heads of state are limited, however, under the Constitution and through democratically elected governments at both federal and state levels. National and state elections are usually held every five years, and all adult citizens are entitled to vote in both. Although the federal government exerts a big influence on Sabah and Sarawak through national development policies, its role is limited in some aspects by the National Constitution, under which certain matters, such as land and forests, fall under state government control. Islam is the official religion of Malaysia, but freedom of religion is guaranteed under the Constitution.

Indonesia

Indonesia is a constitutional republic, having no monarch but a central government which exerts strong control over an enormous, widely scattered and very diverse nation. The president, assisted by a cabinet of ministers, is both head of state and the nation's chief executive. Indonesia has a People's Consultative Assembly and a House of Representatives, both bodies containing democratically elected members. Both also contain appointed representatives from the armed forces, as do the cabinet and local government authorities. The entire nation is divided into provinces, each with its own governor. Under the provincial governors come districts headed by regents, towns headed by mayors, and villages each with their own head. In rural areas, the village head is elected by village members and is therefore in a position to influence the pattern of development according to local conditions. However, all major policy decisions come from central government, which thus has the major influence on the long-term picture of development in Indonesian Borneo.

THE PEOPLE

Borneo's people have long been subject to the tides of history that have brought the powerful influences of customs, cultures and religions from other countries. Yet, so vast is the land, changes absorbed from outside into the lives of a coastal community, for instance, would have had little or no impact on tribes many hundreds of miles away in the interior. On the other hand, internal warfare, shifts in settlement and centuries-old trading relationships have sometimes blurred the distinctions between one people and another.

So, in the 20th century, the ethnic groups of Borneo encompass a broad spectrum that cannot always be divided clearly. Language differences do not always parallel differences in culture. For example, many Borneans share a similar way of life but speak quite different languages, while others share a similar language yet are culturally distinct. There is fertile ground here for research and debate among anthropologists but, unfortunately, also a stumbling-block when it comes to classifying Borneans in unambiguous terms. In many cases, the names now assigned to particular indigenous tribes and groups are, in fact, the names used by *other* tribes and groups, including past colonial administrators. Originally, the people of one particular area or language group did not categorize themselves for the benefit of outsiders but would often adopt the name of their village or a river.

Many names used in the past have fallen into disuse. When reading old books on Borneo, a good deal of detective work may be needed to ascertain to which group of people the author is referring. Names used today may reflect certain characteristics but they are essentially arbitrary. Intermarriage between ethnic and language groups has been commonplace in Borneo since early times. Increasingly, old barriers of distance, language and culture are breaking down. For convenience, however, it is useful to describe five broad categories which encompass the majority of Borneo's people: the mainly Muslim coastal zone communities; the mainly non-Muslim inland farmers; the nomads, or Penan; the Chinese; and other Asian immigrants. Urban communities are a mixture.

It is impossible to give a breakdown of the numbers of people in the ethnic groups of Borneo, and even the total population is in some doubt. Varying sources give different classifications and figures. Putting them all together suggests that there were at least 13 million people in Borneo in 1990, and that the annual increase, from both births and immigration, varies considerably from area to area but lies within the range 2 to 8 per cent. Again, amalgamating data would suggest that about 66 per cent of the total Bornean population is Muslim (mainly coastal, riverside and urban-based), 29 per cent is non-Muslim indigenous (mainly inland farmers and former nomads, plus people who have urban jobs or who work in government service) and 5 per cent Chinese. Only a tiny percentage is nomadic. This rough breakdown conceals considerable regional variation. For example, over 25 per cent of the population in Sarawak is Chinese while only a small minority of the Kalimantan population falls within this grouping. The breakdown also excludes recent Indonesian and Filipino immigrants, mostly in Kalimantan and Sabah, who probably number well over one million.

PEOPLE OF THE COAST

The coastal people of Borneo are predominantly Muslim. They range from fishermen in isolated communities to senior policy-makers in governments. A shared religion and frequent intermarriage over centuries have resulted in continual blending of ethnic and linguistic groups among coastal Muslims. The process has been accelerated in recent years by urban and road development, and by immigrants from neighbouring countries. Increasingly, Muslims of the coastal zone regard themselves firstly as Malays and only secondly as belonging to a particular ethnic or linguistic group. With a few exceptions, the coastal and riverside Muslims of Kalimantan and Sarawak have for long been known as Malays and they do not have distinctive cultural differences from place to place. Their ancestry is a mixture of local natives (especially in West Kalimantan), early non-Muslim immigrants from Java and Sumatra converted to Islam

by traders (especially in South Kalimantan), plus Muslim immigrants over the past five centuries (especially in East Kalimantan). Some Muslim groups take pride, however, in retention of their distinctive cultural identity, and this is particularly evident in Sabah and also northern Sarawak. In these areas, Muslim people retain use of their original languages and like to be referred to by their specific cultural names.

The Suluk

Historically, the dominant group of Muslim coastal and island-dwelling people of north and north-eastern Borneo were the Suluk, who refer to themselves as Tau Sug. They probably originated on the island of Jolo in the southern Philippines, which was the base of the formerly influential Sulu sultanate. Two centuries ago, Suluks dominated trade in the zone encompassing the southern Philippines and north-eastern Borneo. The present-day border between Sabah and the Philippines cuts through the traditional Sulu zone. Social unrest in the southern Philippines in recent decades has stimulated migration of all ethnic groups from this area to Sabah, notably among the numerically dominant Suluks. There is variety in the physical appearance of Suluk people, reflecting their widespread trading and slaving activities of the past. Some, for example, have obvious traces of Arab ancestry. Traditionally, Suluks are noted for their long, airy, colourful clothing.

The East Coast Bajau

On the coast of eastern Borneo and on many of the offshore islands stretching into the Philippines are another grouping commonly known as east coast Bajau. Like the Suluks, historically their distribution was concentrated through north-east Borneo and the southern Philippines. In fact, the so-called east coast Bajau consist of two groups and many sub-groups with different dialects and ways of life. The land or shore-based Bajau Sama are Muslims who have increasingly adopted an urban or agricultural lifestyle in recent decades. The Bajau Laut or Samal are boat-dwellers, mostly non-Muslim, who rarely venture for long onto land, even nowadays. Bajau Laut society consists of family units, one per boat, without formal communal leadership.

Bajau Laut outrigger sailing boats.

Following an essentially nomadic existence, the past role of the Bajau in the coastal economic system in some ways paralleled that of the Penan in the forests. Together with the Suluks, the Bajau Sama and Bajau Laut formed a fascinating interdependent relationship during the 18th and 19th centuries. The Suluks were overall masters of the region. During the period May to November every year, some of the Bajau Sama went on wide-ranging slave-catching expeditions, selling slaves to the wealthy Suluks on their return. Others specialized in manufacturing salt. The process involved making large fires of wood at the sea-side, and repeatedly pouring sea-water on to the fire. This salt was traded with Suluks, who in turn brought it on expeditions to native settlements along the rivers of eastern Borneo, where salt was traded for forest products. Eighteenth-century

European venturers sailing off eastern Borneo observed that the principal activities of the Bajau Laut were fishing, harvesting of sea cucumbers and diving for pearls and mother-of-pearl. Working in groups under the supervision of Suluk masters, the Bajau Laut would dive repeatedly to depths of as much as 15 fathoms (30 metres).

The Idahan, Tidung and Cocos Groups

Around Lahad Datu in eastern Sabah are the Idahan people, who own the rights to collect edible birds' nests from Madai caves. The Idahan claim descent from the earliest Muslim converts in Borneo. Another group of coastal people in south-eastern Sabah and north-eastern Kalimantan are the Tidung. In the 1770s, British adventurer Thomas Forrest noted that the Tidung people living on the lower reaches of rivers in north-east Kalimantan were pagan slave-raiders. Now, presumably through 19th-century contacts with the Sulu sultanate,

the majority are Muslim. The Cocos people of eastern Sabah, now considered natives of the state, are relatively recent arrivals, having come from the Cocos Islands of the Indian Ocean since 1949.

The Orang Sungai

In the 19th century, people in riverside communities of northern Borneo who practised a mixture of hill rice cultivation on the fertile riverside terraces, fishing, hunting and trade, were described by European visitors as Idahan, Eraan, Buludupy, Sabahan and various other names. As a general rule, those living nearest to the sea became Muslims at an early date, and there has been a slow process, still ongoing, of conversion from traditional religions to Islam in the upriver regions. In Sabah, riverine people who do not fit neatly as either coastal Muslims or inland farmers are now called Orang Sungai, meaning 'river people'. The Orang Sungai incorporate speakers of several languages and dialects.

The Bugis

From their homelands in southern Sulawesi, the Muslim Bugis emerged in early historic times as the greatest indigenous seafarers and traders of the South-east Asian archipelago. Moderate in build, both men and women traditionally favour the sarong rather than trousers. Before the first Europeans arrived in the region, the Bugis possessed their own alphabet. Their trading activities covered New Guinea and northern Australia, present-day Indonesia and the Philippines, to mainland South-east Asia. In the 18th century, they had several trading settlements on the east coast of Borneo. At this time, their trade included cloth, foodstuffs, spices, gunpowder, muskets, opium and slaves. In 1726, a Bugis noble conquered Kutai and Pasir in what is now East Kalimantan, and made himself the Sultan of Kutai. Around 1730, Bugis migrants founded Samarinda, now the capital of East Kalimantan. From that period, Bugis traders have penetrated up many of Borneo's east coast rivers and the process continues. In Sabah, where there has been massive immigration of Indonesians in recent decades in response to labour shortages, there are numerous Bugis settlements in both rural and urban areas, and many long-term Bugis residents are considered to be natives.

The Bajau of Kota Belud

The origin of the land-based Bajau people of the coastal plain at Kota Belud in north-western Sabah is something of a mystery. A 19th-century chronicler of Borneo, Spenser St John, uncharitably remarked that 'no one can accuse the Bajau of being a handsome race'. Equally, no one can accuse them of lacking character. They raise and ride horses, and tend herds of cattle and buffaloes. Not surprisingly, they have been dubbed in popular literature as 'the cowboys of the east'. Some believe that they originated as traders from the Malay Peninsula, while others claim connections with the Philippines. There is a story that the horses originated from a shipwreck carrying soldiers of the Mongol empire-builder Kublai Khan, who was expanding his activities into what is now Indonesia around the year AD 1290. More plausibly, horses came to Borneo from the Spanish, via the Philippines. The Bajau people who live fur-

ther south, near the present-day Sabah capital of Kota Kinabalu, do not raise large herds of livestock. Many follow the typical coastal Muslim fishing community tradition of building their houses over the sea.

The Illanun

Living side by side with the Bajau of Kota Belud are the Illanun, also known as Iranun, another coastal Muslim people, who originate from Mindanao in the Philippines. The first main Illanun settlement in Sabah is believed to have occurred in the 1760s, following an enormous volcanic eruption in their homeland. In the early part of the last century, the Illanun were greatly feared as pirates and slave-raiders. Indeed, the Malay term for pirate is *lanun*, which appears to be derivative.

The Brunei Malays

Although history reveals that they represent an ethnic mix, the Brunei Malays are a distinct group in terms of their dialect, array of customs and geographical range. They live only in the coastal parts of Brunei Darussalam, south-western Sabah and northern-most Sarawak. Brunei Malays are strongly religious, yet aspects of their cul-

Children at a Sarawak Malay wedding sing to the accompanying beat of the kompang *(made of stretched goat skin on a wooden hoop).*

ture retain traces of pre-Islamic society. For example, in common with some inland farming groups, they have a hereditary royal family, below which comes a class of noble families related to the sultan, followed by the ordinary people. Formerly mainly fishermen, craftsmen and traders, a large proportion of Brunei Malays now have government jobs in the urban coastal zone. The Muslim Kedayan of Brunei and south-western Sabah are considered to be a different race. Their culture was and still is tied closely to rice cultivation.

The Melanau

These diverse people, related by their use of dialects of the same language group, live in the swampy coastal zone between the lower Rajang and Kemena Rivers in Sarawak. The majority are Muslim but some are Christian or practise their traditional religion. Early European visitors to Borneo reported that the Melanau had a custom of flattening the

A Melanau village at Mukah, Sarawak.

head by applying a wooden device to the forehead of infants. Like most coastal peoples, the Melanau favour a variety of long, loose clothing. By tradition the Melanau are cultivators of sago palm, large areas of which once occupied the coastal swamps of western Borneo. Harvesting and processing is a family-run cottage industry. This palm not only supplies carbohydrate for the growers, but was also one of the major trade items from western Borneo from the times of the early Chinese traders. Tax on Melanau sago helped the Brunei sultanate to flourish. After the Sultan of Brunei ceded territory in northern Sarawak, in the second half of the 19th century, Melanau sago production was again crucial in supporting the Rajah Brooke administration. Even until the late 1940s, sago represented Sarawak's fourth most important revenue earner. But with the trends of mass production of food world-wide after the Second World War, and decreasing prices of starch, the Melanau sago industry has declined drastically.

The non-Muslim Kajang group of the Belaga district share a common ancestry with the Melanau and also have a palm-based traditional economy. A renowned feature of Kajang culture, and also of the Melanau, is their custom of burying the dead in a chamber on top of massive, carved ironwood poles (known as *keliring* in Kajang and *jerunai* in Melanau) erected near the village centre.

INLAND FARMERS

The complexity of languages, dialects and cultures of the inland farmers means that no one classification is entirely appropriate. The generic term Dayaks, or Dyaks, was adopted by European explorers in the 19th century to refer to the non-Muslim farmers of interior Borneo and is still current in the four Kalimantan provinces. Indeed, it has become popular among these peoples as a name that signifies their desire to retain their diverse cultural heritage in a nation which is predominantly Muslim and in many ways is becoming more homogeneous. The term is less frequently used in Sarawak and has never been recognized in Sabah. However, its common usage disguises the fact that Dayaks comprise several quite distinct peoples.

Based on similarities in language and culture, seven major groups of inland farmers can be identified: the Iban (previously known as Sea Dayaks); the Bidayuh (Land Dayaks); the Kayan-Kenyah group; the Maloh; the Barito; the Kelabit-Lun Bawang group; and the Dusun-Kadazan-Murut group. Several of these groups overlap in their distribution in central Borneo, as a result of repeated intertribal warfare and migrations in the past, and there are also

Above: *Iban longhouse with palm-thatch roof and walls incorporating wood, bark and bamboo.*

Right: *Arriving at a longhouse on the upper Rajang River. Muddy feet are washed before climbing the stairway to the building which is sited above flood level on a fertile riverside terrace.*

Opposite: *Meal time for the men in the large communal area of a longhouse. Steamed rice is served in banana-leaf packets. The bowls contain meat and fish dishes.*

many smaller groups. The great majority of these farming peoples traditionally have an economy based on cultivation of hill rice, though a few cultivated sago palms or planted irrigated rice prior to this century.

Longhouses

Nearly all these communities once lived in longhouses. Up to 300 metres (1,000 feet) long, raised on posts as much as 12 metres (40 feet) above the ground and housing over 100 families, the longhouse made sense in the periods of warfare of past centuries, as it could function as a fort. Nowadays, though generally smaller and set on shorter posts, longhouses still retain their traditional framework, with separate rooms providing a degree of privacy for each family and a large communal area where all the social activities of the group take place.

While some groups have consistently retained large longhouses as a central part of their culture, others have largely or entirely abandoned this system in favour of a separate house for each family. In Sabah and Sarawak, this has perhaps been a result of the relatively peaceful conditions which have prevailed since the late 19th century, as there was never any pressure from government to abandon the longhouse system. In Kalimantan, the government of the 1950s and 1960s tended to encourage individual houses, but since the late 1970s there has been increasing official support for retention of longhouses.

Tour operators have not been slow to recognize the appeal of longhouses, many of which are now reasonably accessible either overland or by river. Although much of the old way of life may be looked for in vain, a visitor who takes care to observe the usual courtesies can expect hospitality and perhaps the chance to stay overnight.

Traditional Beliefs of the Inland Groups

The traditional religions of inland farmers are varied but generally involve belief in the existence of good and evil spirits. Many groups also believe in omens, notably that the calls and movements of certain wild birds give warnings as to courses of action to be taken. Various aspects of the cultures, such as woodcarvings, are closely tied to

Some highland peoples of central Borneo built elaborate tombs for high-ranking members of their communities. Called salong, *these wooden tomb huts are raised on massive pillars and intricately carved and painted.*

religious beliefs. Headhunting, banned and eventually stopped by European governments of the 19th and early 20th centuries, was of major religious significance to some groups. Kalimantan Dayaks in various areas converted to Christianity during the period of Dutch rule, but this situation changed after the Second World War. In Indonesia, the official state policy of *Pancasila* requires that all citizens believe in one supreme God. However, the policy involves a good deal of flexibility and the Kaharingan faith of the Dayaks of southern Borneo, basically the traditional religion of the Ngaju group with elements of Bali Hindu and Christianity, is accepted by the government of Indonesia. Many conversions to Christianity occurred in Sarawak and Sabah after the Second World War. Fewer communities of inland farmers have converted to Islam, in part because of a continuing reliance in remoter communities on species of wild animals forbidden to Muslims, for protein and fat requirements.

The Iban

The Iban are the largest inland farming group in Borneo. Seemingly confined to the upper Kapuas River in the mid-16th century, they expanded fairly slowly into southern Sarawak up to about 1800. Throughout the 19th century there was a period of massive, vigorous northwards expansion through the Rajang drainage up to the lower Baram River. During the 20th century, Iban communities continued to move into the northern part of Sarawak and Brunei Darussalam. The Sarawak Iban population is relatively new, therefore, and culturally homogeneous. The Kalimantan population consists of an array of older, more varied communities including the Kantu, Sebruang, Bugau, Mualang and Desa. Early European commentators frequently drew attention to the fine features of the Iban. Typical are the words of Hugh Low: '. . . with fine limbs of excellent proportions; a subdued and calm, but resolute air . . . walking with a light and graceful step . . .'. The long hair and filed teeth also noted by early visitors to Borneo are things of the past, and body tattoos almost so.

The reasons for the great expansion of Ibans into Sarawak continue to baffle anthropologists. A key element seems to be that Iban society is egalitarian, unlike many other Borneo societies, placing high value on individual striving, physical courage and endeavour; young men are expected to travel extensively before settling. Although many Ibans are now Christians, traditional beliefs and customs remain important. These include reverence for legendary heroes and deities, story-telling, belief in bird omens (the hornbill is regarded as sacred) and annual festivals (*gawai*) involving traditional costumes, dancing and drinking of rice wine.

The Bidayuh

The Bidayuh of southern Sarawak and northern West Kalimantan are a heterogeneous group linked by a similar language. Like the Iban, they have an egalitarian society, but one which traditionally placed much less prominence on ostentation or militarism. Quiet pragmatism was their strong feature. Some communities had individual, closely spaced houses while others had longhouses which were small by Borneo standards. In the past, a common feature of Bidayuh villages was a central community building – known as *baruk* – used by the men for discussion, story-telling, entertaining, trading, ceremonies, dispute-settling, and making and repairing personal possessions.

The Kayan-Kenyah Group

According to their own beliefs, handed down by word of mouth over many generations, the homeland of the Kayan-Kenyah group was the Apo Kayan region of East Kalimantan. During the 18th and 19th centuries, the Kayan split and moved in all directions, including into Sarawak, the Mahakam River and Kapuas River. There are now many widely scattered Kayan communities which retain very similar language and culture. Physically, both Kayan and Kenyah are typically pale-skinned with a broad face. Older women usually have pierced earlobes, stretched distinctively through wearing heavy metal earrings. Included within the Kayan group are the Modang of the Mahakam River and the Segai of north-east Kalimantan, now a peaceful minority tribe who were feared as far north as the Kinabatangan River in Sabah in the mid-19th century for their fierce raiding expeditions.

The Kenyah are much more varied than the Kayan in their language and details of their culture. Their origins are obscure, but the upper Kayan River region would seem to be most likely. They replaced the Kayan people as the dominant group of the Apo Kayan region, probably in the early 19th century, but Kenyah villages exist throughout northern interior Borneo.

The Kayan and Kenyah once had an extremely feudal society consisting of two classes of nobles, one or two classes of commoners, and slaves. Status was inherited. The commoners, numerically dominant, were obliged to provide free labour and goods for the higher classes, while the higher classes were expected to manage the protection and spiritual welfare of the community. The feudal nature of Kayan-Kenyah societies has softened greatly during this century, along with the abolition of slavery and introduction of Christianity. The Kayan and Kenyah longhouse is a solid, carefully constructed and very impressive structure, at least 2 metres (7 feet) off the ground on massive ironwood pillars, with ironwood shingles for the roof.

In the lower Baram area of northern

A woman of the Kayan-Kenyah group. The stretched earlobes, a traditional mark of beauty and status, are rarely seen in younger women.

Sarawak are the Berawan group of communities, who are considered to be allied to the Kenyah. Intermediate between Kayan and Kenyah are the Ngurek, who traditionally cut stone mausoleums for their dead.

The Maloh

The Maloh or Embaloh group, including the Taman and Kalis sub-groups, together known as Banuaka in their home territory of interior West Kalimantan, have a stratified society. Even in the past, when inland Bornean communities tended to migrate quite often, the Maloh were relatively settled people, who grew rice in the extensive flatlands of the upper Kapuas and were the main indigenous traders of this part of Borneo. Many of the Maloh group specialized in skilled artistry with metals and beads, as well as painting and woodcarving. In the past, those skilled at working silver and gold were the only communities which formed mutually beneficial relationships with the Ibans who lived in the same region.

The Barito

The so-called Barito group includes an array of people whose distribution encompasses most of Central Kalimantan and adjacent parts of interior West, South and East

Kalimantan. Numerically, the largest component are the Ngaju followed by the Ot Danum. Others include Tamoan, Sabuang, Ma'anyan, Lawangan, Bukit, Tunjung, Benuaq, Bentian, Siang, Murung, Tebidah, Kebahan and Limbai. The Barito peoples are variable in physical appearance and in their adornments but, both traditionally and now, they often favour colourful and somewhat ostentatious clothing and decorations. Most groups live in longhouses and traditionally had a stratified society. All have complex death rituals, often involving sacrifice of a buffalo or pig (in the past, a slave) at carved ironwood poles. Some have secondary funerals where bones or ashes are stored in large jars or in special tombs. Both the spiritual and related material aspects of their culture are varied and rich. A large proportion of the group practise the Kaharingan religion.

The Kelabit-Lun Bawang Group

This group occupies a region which has as its centre the meeting zone of Sarawak, East Kalimantan, Sabah and Brunei. Communities in the Kelabit Highlands of Sarawak and the Kerayan Highlands of East Kalimantan long ago developed systems for irrigation of wet rice on infertile sandy valley soils, independently of wet rice development in coastal swamps elsewhere in Borneo. The sturdy people of these remote regions, many of whom have fine faces full of character, also acquired buffaloes at a relatively early stage in their history, and developed the practice of making salt from natural mineral springs long ago, thereby making them less reliant than the other interior Bornean groups on trade with coastal people. The Lun Bawang section of this group inhabits the lower, coastal parts of northern Sarawak. In East Kalimantan and Sabah, these people are known as Lun Dayeh.

The Dusun-Kadazan-Murut Group

The group may be viewed as closely allied, because their languages are related to those of the southern Philippines and because their distribution falls fairly neatly into the area occupied by Sabah. In Sabah, however, the Dusuns and Kadazans are regarded as distinct from the Muruts, who are confined to the south-west and Sabah-

Rungus woman from Kudat, wearing the coiled copperware and beads traditionally favoured by the people of this Dusun group.

cieties is stratified and they do not favour ostentatious material objects, although many communities traditionally put a high value on ancient Chinese stoneware jars and brass gongs.

Other Inland Groups

There are many other numerically small groups which do not fit neatly into the above classification. Among the largest of these are the Bisaya, who in Brunei Darussalam and the lowlands of northern Sarawak are mainly non-Muslims, while those in south-western Sabah are Muslim. Both Muslim and non-Muslim Bisaya are relatively settled people, who traditionally lived in individual family houses, grew wet rice and sago palms from early times, and have medicine men and women. Muslim and non-Muslim Bisaya believe that the original king of Brunei was of their race, yet in modern Brunei they are known as Dusun or Bukit.

THE NOMADIC PENAN

The inland forests of Borneo have long been home to nomadic hunter-gatherers. These distinctively light-skinned people, typically slender, not especially muscular or robust, at first glance seem ill-adapted to life in rough, remote forests. Traditionally, their clothing is very sparse, and affords no protection against the spines, buttresses and rocks which continually scrape the inexperienced forest traveller. Borneo forest nomads are now commonly known as Penan or Punan, but other names such as Bukit, Bukat, Bekatan, Ukit and Ot are also used. Most groups which were once nomadic have become partially or entirely settled as farmers, a community typically containing between 15 and 75 persons. In Sarawak, less than 4 per cent of the state's 10,000 or so Penan are now entirely nomadic. The common feature of Penan is that they live off the forest for all or part of the time, not that they represent a single language or cultural group.

One of the curious aspects of the Penan is their distribution in Borneo. They live essentially in the central hilly regions, encompassing Sarawak, Brunei Darussalam, East Kalimantan and the interior parts of West and Central Kalimantan, but not in

Kalimantan border regions. Overall, this group includes communities which live along lowland rivers and on plains, and up through steep hill ranges to 1,300 metres (4,300 feet) on the southern slopes of Gunung Kinabalu. Except along the west coast plains, hill rice is still favoured over wet rice. Amongst the Dusuns and Kadazans, individual houses were already replacing longhouses by the time of the first

European contacts, while longhouses were still normal for most Murut communities until recent decades.

The Rungus people of the northern tip of Sabah are unique within the Dusun-Kadazan group in still building longhouses and in using beads and copperware as major features of their ornamentation. Two centuries ago, their territory was one of the major sources of Bornean camphor, but the landscape has since become one of secondary forests and *lallang* grass, probably because the area has a highly seasonal rainfall pattern and has long been subject to droughts and forest fires.

None of the Dusun-Kadazan-Murut so-

Sabah, and barely south of the equator. To some extent, their distribution is limited by that of the hill sago palm on which they rely – or, if settled, on which their ancestors relied – as a major constituent of their diet. There also seems to be some connection with the distribution of the Kayan-Kenyah group, which is among the most ancient of Bornean lines, and with whom the Penan have close traditional trading links.

The harvesting of the hill sago palm is typical of the Penan philosophy of long-term sustainable use of plant products within the territory of the community. The palm grows in clumps of several stems. The Penan cut only one or two stems from a clump at one time, thereby ensuring that the plant will not die and will produce new stems to provide food for future generations. As the plant tends to grow profusely in certain localities, many stems can be harvested at one time in one locality, providing two sorts of food. From those that have not yet flowered, the leaf bud, relatively soft and containing both protein and carbohydrate, is cut and eaten. From stems that have begun to flower, starch is obtained. In this case, the felled stems are cut into sections about a metre long, which are carried, pushed and rolled to a processing platform built next to a stream. Here, the pith is chopped, washed and pressed to extract starch.

The ideas of a beautiful, clean environment and of minimizing the need for tedious hard work are central to the Penan's love of his or her lifestyle, and are attainable by living with the forest, not by replacing it. A Penan community regards any useful tree within its range of activity as belonging to the community, or to the individual who first found the tree. Apart from a clump of sago palms, a useful tree is typically one which produces edible fruits or is a source of medicines. Unlike their treatment of plants, the Penan's harvesting of animal resources is generally not done in a consciously sustainable manner – a hunter will go for any animal, but large ones are almost invariably preferred to small.

Penan trails – like those of other Bornean interior people – follow ridges where possible, because ridges provide the easiest walking. A trail is maintained whenever a Penan walks along it, by the cutting of saplings, branches and lianas. These cuts

can be read as a code by others following the trail later, guiding their steps or telling them of events that occurred previously. Of key importance to the Penan in describing their landscape, and in knowing how not to get lost, are the rivers and streams. Names of watercourses are derived from past events in the catchment, such as the death of a hunting dog. Even tiny streams have a name, so that directions and routes can be described by a Penan to other members of his or her group. The relative size, direction of flow and quality of a watercourse all provide useful information, as do features of land topography between streams, proximity to the headwaters and position of landmarks such as rocks. To a Penan, the forest is a complex array of possessions, historical events and opportunities set in a matrix.

The Penan's concept of *stewardship* of land and forest as a whole, and *ownership* of specific trees, is difficult to reconcile with the way in which most modern societies manage natural resources. Typically, the view of governments is that individuals may be granted ownership of land where the forest has been replaced with an alternative use, while land under natural forest is viewed as state-owned. Thus, any trees which happen to be on that land are the property of the government. The treatment of the Penan by governments is commonly misunderstood. The government view, which is supported by historical evidence, is that the remaining nomadic Penan should

A Penan woman with her child in a baby-carrier woven from split rattan stems.

and will eventually become settled farmers. In fact, the majority of Penan communities have become partially or entirely settled during the 20th century, not as a result of planned government schemes, but voluntarily. This is not to say that Penan settlement is automatically without problems. In some cases, the worry that they will become landless paupers has turned into reality.

In a Sarawak government workshop on Penan development held in 1991, an analysis of various Penan settlements showed that there are three main prerequisites for successful adoption of a settled existence by nomadic Penan. They are secure and exclusive tenure of a specific land area; freedom of the community to decide on its own course of development; and cordial, learning relationships with their non-Penan neighbours.

Another government view is that the Penan form only a tiny minority of the people of central Borneo and that logging, which provides enormous revenue for overall development of the entire population, is a more rational option than retaining large forest areas for a minority. However, the government of Sarawak has allocated several specific forest areas for nomadic Penan.

THE CHINESE
AND OTHER ASIAN IMMIGRANTS

Chinese contacts with Borneo date back more than a thousand years but the first significant settlement of Chinese immigrants was near Sambas in West Kalimantan between 1750 and 1820 to work the goldfields there. Chinese immigration was always allowed, and sometimes encouraged, both by the Brookes in Sarawak and by the British North Borneo administration until the time of independence. The most numerous Chinese groups in Borneo are the Hakka, Foochow, Cantonese, Hokkien and Teochew, who are all predominantly Buddhist, Taoist or Christian. Although the Chinese occupy a wide variety of roles in Borneo, it is in the fields of trade and commerce that they have excelled and made their reputation.

Among other Asian immigrants, the Javanese have the longest history of contact with Borneo. They had started coming to Borneo by the 14th century, during the time of the Majapahit empire. Now, people of Javanese origin may be found all over Kalimantan and also in Sabah and Sarawak. In recent decades, there has been planned immigration of Javanese into Kalimantan under the Indonesian government's pro-

gramme of transmigration to agricultural schemes. There is also a predominance of recent Javanese immigrants among manual workers in the petroleum and timber-based industries in Kalimantan. Also in the southern third of the island of Borneo are many Madurese immigrants, so-called 'spontaneous' migrants, who have come from the Indonesian island of Madura, independently of government-sponsored schemes. They work in both urban and rural areas in a variety of unskilled and semi-skilled jobs.

Small numbers of Indians entered and

Sibu town, Sarawak, three decades ago.

have stayed in Sarawak and Sabah since the late 19th century, as a result of British influence in these states. In Sabah, there are two other groups of immigrants which have been arriving in large numbers only in recent decades and which have had significant impacts on the state's economic development. Christian Filipinos occupy skilled positions where command of English is important, both in Sabah and also Brunei. The trend of immigration in this group started in the mid-1950s, when the introduction of mechanized logging by American and British companies in what was then British North Borneo brought about a need for skilled machine operators able to speak English. Many of the children of this first wave of Filipino immigrants are now Malaysian citizens. A more recent influx into Sabah has been that of people from the islands of eastern Indonesia. Many Sabahans own small land-holdings which they do not work at themselves because of better opportunities in towns. Hardy immigrants from the islands of Timor, Flores and Buton have readily found jobs in these and other situations. For all these people of non-Bornean origin, the presence of relatives already in Borneo is an important factor in stimulating more migrants to come from their place of origin.

A Sarawak Chinese goldsmith at work.

BORNEO'S CULTURAL HERITAGE

Borneo's people have a proud heritage of culture and art that lies deeply rooted in the past, enriched by the crafts, customs and religions that have filtered down through the centuries from China, mainland Asia and the surrounding islands of Indonesia and the Philippines. In their festivities and ceremonies, their craftsmanship, their homes, even in their clothes and ornaments, Borneans have traditionally celebrated their affinity with the land, the growing and harvesting of rice, and the events that have shaped and directed their lives.

FESTIVALS

Public festivals are held throughout the year in Borneo to mark such holidays as the Chinese New Year or major events in the Christian or Muslim calendars. There are many local festivals, too, for instance to celebrate the beginning and end of harvests or the end of a period of mourning for the dead. These occasions are usually a time for dressing up, feasting, dancing and the performance of traditional games and ceremonies involving an entire community. Non-Bornean visitors are often warmly encouraged to join in and, in non-Muslim communities, plied with vast quantities of rice wine.

Chinese New Year prayers at a temple in Sarawak.

DANCE AND MUSIC

Ethnic dances, still performed on special occasions or perhaps simply when a longhouse community throws a party, are highly symbolic, portraying the feats of great warriors – for which participants will wear full war-dress – the thrills of the hunt or the gathering in of the harvest. The older generations, especially, are familiar with every movement, having seen and learnt these dances, with their stylized rhythms and rituals, over a lifetime. Singing often accompanies the dancing, with music played on such traditional instruments as gongs, drums and guitars. In fact, some Borneans are not only good musicians but skilled instrument-makers, too, crafting flutes from bamboo and stringed instruments such as lutes from a single piece of wood.

ARTS AND CRAFTS

Weaving

Until comparatively recently, the materials for woven goods such as clothing, blankets and wall-hangings came entirely from the forest. Wild cotton was picked, processed and spun by hand; leaves and fruits provided the rich colours used to dye the finished cloth in a variety of stylized patterns; and bark was peeled from trees to make stout jackets that could be painted, stencilled or decorated with beads. The Iban, in particular, were renowned for their cloth-making and tie-dyeing, the skills being handed from mothers to daughters down the generations.

Basketry

Intricately plaited baskets, huge shady hats and colourful mats are not only the most popular handicrafts sought by tourists but are also highly practical items, widely used among Borneo's ethnic groups. Most are made from split rattan stems, which are both pliable and durable.

Beadwork

Beads have long been valuable among Bornean tribes, in the past for barter but also for personal adornment indicating wealth and status within the community. Women of some indigenous groups traditionally used glass beads as lavish additions to their festive costumes, painstakingly working them into hats, headbands, jackets and collars in a multitude of colours and shapes. Beadwork frequently appears on other items such as decorative baskets, bags and small household goods.

Woodcarving

This art has a strong religious significance, as shown by the symbols and motifs carved on longhouses, coffins, burial chambers and the long poles that once stood at the entrance to nearly every rural village to ward off evil spirits. The patterns of birds – particularly the hornbill – dragons and other fantastic creatures also appear on warshields, ceremonial masks and even mundane agricultural tools, offering protection or calling the attention of appropriate deities to their users. Genuine old woodcarvings are rarely found on the open market and most of the artefacts offered for sale to tourists are modern facsimiles.

Metalwork

Locally cast metals were once part of a thriving industry in Borneo. Brass, lead and silver were used for firearms, tools and domestic items, and for creating beautiful earrings, headdresses and coin ornaments for ceremonial wear. The Dayak tribes had an excellent reputation as skilled swordsmiths. The iron that they used for making swords, jungle knives and blowpipes was largely obtained through barter with foreign traders, although iron ore was once mined in certain highland locations in Borneo. Nowadays, jungle knives and other iron tools are fashioned from the springs of old trucks and from chainsaw blades.

Tattooing

Tattooing must be the ultimate form of personal ornamentation. Though rarely seen among younger Borneans, it was the custom in the past for both men and women to decorate their bodies in this way. They had to undergo many painful hours as the tattooist used needles to punch in ink, usually made from a mixture of soot and *damar* (hard, crystalline tree resin). The patterns, to symbolize bravery or enhance beauty, varied from tribe to tribe and, in some cases, a person's social standing had to be recognized before tattooing was allowed.

Left: *Young Bidayuh women, wearing traditional conical hats of woven rattan.*

Below: *One of the special features of the Iban group of peoples is their textile weaving, involving designs that carry religious or social meanings. Here, an Iban woman weaves a* pua kumbu, *a decorative cloth demanding the highest skill. Note, too, the massive jars in the background, which serve both for storage purposes and as heirlooms.*

Opposite left: *Iban women demonstrate their home-woven skirts with traditional motifs and other finery reserved for special occasions.*

Opposite right: *Funerary poles (*keliring*), consisting of carved ironwood tree trunks, traditionally commemorated the death of great leaders in northern central Borneo.*

Opposite below: *Body tattoos, of various designs, normally served either to mark personal achievement or to ward off disease. The patterns were tapped into the skin, usually periodically over many years, using soot mixed with* damar *(tree resin).*

TRADITIONAL ECONOMY

Although modern industry is changing Borneo, a considerable proportion of the population still relies on the land for existence. For many communities, traditional methods of agriculture, fishing and hunting have stood the test of time and are used in much the same way as they were centuries ago. Considerations such as travel, finding food and making the best use of available forest products are not always easy to address even in the 20th century, and earlier societies needed much resilience and ingenuity to derive a precarious living from the forest.

The capacity of the natural Bornean rainforest to support people is very low. Without agriculture or trade, a hunting and gathering community in any one area cannot possibly grow very large. Consequently, the earliest human communities in Borneo must have suffered from periods of famine and the need to move to new areas.

Excavations at Niah and Madai caves have shown that Bornean people many thousands of years ago consumed a variety of mammals (especially wild pigs, rodents, monkeys and apes including the Orangutan), birds, reptiles, fish and molluscs. Plant materials do not last long in the tropics, so it cannot be said how much they featured in prehistoric human diets. Possibly wild hill sago palms were harvested. Edible fruits, seeds and mushrooms are surprisingly seasonal in Bornean rainforest, so at most times of the year, and in most places, there is almost no wild plant material edible to humans. Natural fluctuations in sea level must have influenced what was available in coastal areas.

SALT

Probably one of the factors limiting where early humans could live in Borneo would have been access to salt. In the humid tropics, any physical activity causes sweating and loss of salt from the body, which is not easy to replace in areas where the small quantities of salt that exist naturally in the environment are continually leached away by heavy rainfall. Early societies would have been compelled to live not far from the sea or from natural inland salt sources, for at least part of the time. The salt problem would have persisted with the development of agriculture, and would have been overcome only with regular trade. The early coastal trading chiefdoms and sultanates must have been able to exert bargaining

---

A Kadazan farmer of western Sabah distributes bundles of rice seedlings ready for planting out in irrigated fields.

power over people of the interior by controlling human traffic, and hence salt supplies. Interestingly, there are natural sources of salt in several remote areas of Borneo where there have been human communities for a very long time.

RICE

Exactly how and when agriculture arose in Borneo is unknown. Borrowing from our knowledge of trends in the development of agriculture in the South-east Asian region as a whole, around 3000 BC would be a likely starting period. Nowadays, all foods other than rice are regarded merely as supplements by most Bornean people outside urban areas. Rice is *the* staple food. The average rural Bornean eats about 170 kilograms (370 pounds) of uncooked rice annually. An adult working man may consume well over 200 kilograms (440 pounds). Cooked, the rice weighs up to three times this amount. It is by no means certain, however, that common rice – a native of northeastern India and southern China – was the first major agricultural crop in Borneo. Possibly wild hill sago or the swamp sago from eastern Indonesia was planted first. Some carbohydrate crops now important in rural Borneo came much more recently. Among these are corn, sweet potato and tapioca, all from America and introduced through European explorers.

Ancient Bornean communities must have struggled hard to elevate rice to its current supreme importance in the rural economy and, thereby, in society and in the traditional landscape. The original wild rice from mainland Asia requires climatic conditions which do not occur in Borneo, notably a distinct seasonality in rainfall. Thus, early farmers must have cultivated and selected rice over very many generations in order to breed varieties which could cope with Borneo's varied terrain, soil conditions and wet climate. There are now many varieties, some capable of tolerating poor soils better than others. Some produce a lot of rather tasteless grains, while others produce smaller quantities of tasty, large grains.

A second reason why rice is likely to have got off to a slow start as a major food crop in Borneo is that it can be grown only in open conditions, clear of tree cover, which

normally requires the felling of many large, hardwood trees. This is difficult to achieve without metal axes which, on available evidence, probably appeared in Borneo well after 500 BC.

There are two basic ways of growing rice. 'Wet' rice needs to grow in fields of water. Early wet rice was grown in natural swamps, as are some varieties today. In most cases, however, the water is obtained by diverting watercourses or capturing and retaining rainfall. Wet rice can be grown only on flat land or where the land can be made flat by terracing and the water retained by small dams. 'Dry' or 'hill' rice is sustained only by rain, and can be grown on both flat land and on slopes, including steep hillsides. Some communities grow only wet rice, some only dry, and some both kinds.

To the grower, there are advantages and disadvantages to both methods. Successful cultivation of wet rice involves more work but depends less on the vagaries of weather, produces a higher yield per area of land and has the key advantage that most weeds are suppressed by the presence of water. In rural areas where there is no shortage of land, however, farmers may see no merit in maximizing yields in terms of land area used and prefer to grow hill rice, which requires less labour and produces tastier grains. Their biggest problem is to suppress weeds which, in the humid tropics, grow more rapidly and continuously than under any other conditions. The easiest way to minimize weed problems is to grow dry rice on forest land – where herbaceous weeds are virtually absent – by felling and burning the trees as soon as the wood is sufficiently dry.

SHIFTING CULTIVATION

As the growing of hill rice is linked to felling of forest, the cultivators of hill rice – commonly labelled 'shifting cultivators' or 'swidden farmers' – are often blamed for deforestation, especially by foresters. In fact, the situation is by no means as simple as this. For a start, shifting cultivators generally prefer to grow rice on land which has grown rice previously and where, in the meantime, secondary forest has grown up, one reason being that the trees are small and relatively easy to fell. Also, studies in

Hill farmers planting rice. Due to frequent rain, the felled secondary forest often does not burn well, but enough to provide weed-free space and fertilizing ash. The men make holes with sharpened stakes while the women follow and plant the seeds.

the Bahau Valley in East Kalimantan suggest that soils under secondary forests may be more suitable for growing rice than soils under old growth forest. Shifting cultivators leave a rice field because its fertility has been sapped by growth and harvesting, and because weeds have become uncontrollable. They know, however, that it is vital that conditions when they leave are right for secondary forest to grow up again. This means that rice fields always have to be near to forest, so that there is a natural source of tree seeds to recolonize the abandoned field. This, in turn, means that traditional shifting cultivation is done in an environment where forest is always preserved. In practice, stable shifting cultivation results in a series of rice fields in a continuous but ever-changing patchwork of secondary plant growth.

Traditional shifting cultivators usually prefer to concentrate rice fields on the fertile alluvial terraces along rivers and on the lower slopes of hills. As far as possible, the infertile higher slopes and ridge tops are left

under the original forest. So, the majority of traditional shifting cultivators cannot be blamed as a significant cause of loss of pristine forests.

Low-intensity shifting cultivation allows some plant and animal species which are not adapted to the conditions of undisturbed forests to thrive. Such plants are often favoured foods of large mammals desired for meat, such as deer and wild cattle. Also, shifting cultivators plant various wild fruit trees, thereby boosting the natural populations of these valuable plants and providing future food supplies for wildlife. Unfortunately, this generally stable system has broken down in some areas and is now rapidly collapsing in many parts of Borneo.

LAND AND FOREST TENURE

All economies require a communally accepted system of tenure over land and resources, so that natural commodities are not exhausted by unregulated exploitation and so that people who devote effort to producing a resource do not run the risk of seeing it hijacked. This simple truth applies in rural Borneo as much as anywhere else. The failure of people from outside rural communities to recognize it represents a key to understanding the various conflicts and deteriorating quality of land use that are seen in many parts of Borneo.

When a man fells old growth forest for farming, usually assisted by family members and close friends, he acquires rights to that land. Virtually all traditional communities in Borneo recognize his authority to cultivate the land in the future, or pass authority on to his descendants. Rights to any trees he plants are also retained by him and his descendants.

Traditional communities regard surrounding old growth forest as their possession. The boundaries of community land are delimited and communally accepted, but are not apparent to outsiders because they are not marked on the ground or on any maps. Community members normally seek approval from others before felling old growth forest within the limits. Within any old growth forest there may be trees over which particular individuals or families hold sole rights to use. Such trees are usually either those favoured by wild honey-bees or species which produce edible fruits or other harvestable products. These rights will usually have been acquired by the first finder of the tree.

Many communities traditionally retained patches of old growth forest fairly near to the community centre, within large tracts of fallow land under secondary forest. These patches are marked by various features. They may be steep land unsuitable for cultivation, places where there is a spring of water, places with unusual rock formations or massive strangling figs, or with an abundance of wild fruit trees. In many cases, these forest patches are associated with the existence of spirits.

FISHING AND HUNTING

Fish, both freshwater and marine, are relished by almost all communities and a variety of fishing methods are used, mainly nets, traps and natural plant poisons. Most communities claim the right for any community member to fish within delimited stretches of river, but exclude non-community members.

Hunting is a major source of food for inland communities. Bearded pigs and deer are normally favoured and the usual technique is to use dogs to locate the prey, which is dispatched with a spear. Shotguns are now widely used by hunters in Sabah

Iban men with their dogs on a hunting expedition.

and Sarawak, while use of the blowpipe, formerly favoured for obtaining monkeys, hornbills and other tree-dwelling animals, is decreasing and has been entirely abandoned in many areas. Rights to hunting are typically looser than rights to land, forest and fishing, but a hunter will normally seek permission to hunt in individually owned land and will not stray into the forest land of another community.

TRAVEL

People used to travel in Borneo either on foot or in a wooden dug-out boat. Even nowadays, when life is not nearly so tough as in past times, if a native of the hilly interior and a physically fit visitor to Borneo start walking a forest trail at the same instant, the former will normally be way ahead and out of sight within half a minute, and will have reached his destination in under half the time taken by the latter.

Both stamina and practice, ideally from early childhood, are needed to keep moving at a steady pace on constantly uneven ground, dodging never-ceasing stumps, roots, logs, buttresses, branches and dangling vegetation, all the while cutting away the most obstructive bits with deft swipes of a *parang* (a long knife, the most essential tool for travellers in Bornean forests). Seasoned natives of the interior can hump loads of several tens of kilograms over rough terrain, traditionally in long, tubular baskets or rattan frames, with shoulder and head straps made of tree bark. But there are limits to the amount that a person can carry on his or her back.

The introduction of buffaloes and horses into parts of Borneo, probably a few hundreds of years ago, made life slightly easier for some people, but neither beast is particularly useful in the highly uneven, typically grassless terrain and humid conditions which characterize Borneo. In the early 20th century, the British North Borneo Company developed a system of bridle paths to link remote settlements, many of which remained in use until after the Second World War. Horses were used to carry expatriate officers and supplies but the paths had no significant effect on the distribution of human settlement or on volume and type of trade.

Boats were normally used wherever that would be quicker than walking. This was most often the case when large amounts of belongings or forest produce had to be moved over long distances. Rivers, then, were once the main highways and means of communication and villages grew up along their banks. Anything that could be put in a dug-out canoe or on a bamboo raft was moved around in that way. Where there were rapids, the boats were pushed, pulled and manoeuvred through. Where there were waterfalls, or crossings over ridges dividing watersheds, the contents of the boat were taken out, and the whole lot plus boat would be carried or dragged through the forest to the nearest navigable point.

TRADE

Although many Bornean communities were self-sufficient in food under the traditional economy and some produced their own tools from locally obtained iron, almost all traded to supply other needs. Metal tools became essential throughout Borneo for forest clearance and farming, for house construction, for making hunting implements and for head-hunting. Imported ceramics came in various forms and provided kitchen utensils, storage jars (for drinking-water, rice, rice wine and human bones), ornaments and valuable heirlooms and dowry gifts. The expression 'beads for the natives' is now used whimsically, but imported high-quality coloured beads were indeed a highly valued item for some Bornean peoples, whose ceremonial ornamentation and relative wealth was judged by possession of beads, both loose and in the form of necklaces, caps and girdles. Diamonds and gold were the only precious minerals that were traded in significant quantities from Borneo in the old days.

Until the early part of this century, many rural Borneans relied on pounded tree bark and cloth woven from local plant fibres to fashion their daily clothing. Ceremonial dress incorporated animal skins, feathers and teeth. Nevertheless, today's situation, where even the remotest inhabitants of Borneo wear imported, mass-produced clothes, is the culmination of a trend in importation of cloth that started generations ago.

Marine produce, collected primarily off north and east Borneo and traded with the Chinese, included dried sea cucumbers or holothurians (known among the traders as *tripang* or *Bêche-de-mer*), sharks' fins, mother-of-pearl and pearls.

Bornean forest plants and animals yielded numerous items formerly collected in large quantities by inland peoples and traded with coastal communities who in turn traded them mainly with the Chinese and also Indians, Arabs and Europeans. Rattan and hardwoods formed a part of the trade in early times but more important were products of trees which fetched high prices for relatively small quantities. Among these, resins and seeds from dipterocarp trees were significant items. *Damar* was used for caulking boats, in the manufacture of varnish and buttons, and was burned for light. And one of the most important early items of trade from Borneo to China, as well as to India and later probably Arabia, was camphor, the aromatic resin of the Kapur tree (the Borneo camphorwood), one of the largest dipterocarp trees in the lowland and hill forests of Borneo. This extremely valuable substance, used in medicines, was known to the Chinese as 'dragon's brain'.

Illipe nuts (the seeds of several *Shorea* tree species, which contain high concentrations of a viscous oil) were used locally as a cooking oil and exported for manufacture of lubricating oil and wax. Even now, illipe nuts are collected and exported for use in expensive chocolates and cosmetics.

In the 19th century, gutta-percha became an important forest product from Borneo entering international trade. This was a latex from *Palaquium* trees, which softens when heated and hardens when cooled, used in the manufacture of riding whips, coating for telegraphic and early electrical cables, surgical instruments, golf balls and adhesive. *Gaharu* was and remains another rare and valuable forest product. This blackish, fragrant growth (also known as aloeswood or eaglewood), caused by fungal attack, is sometimes found in the trunk of two or three tree species of the family Thymelaeaceae and is much prized as scent.

Wild animals contributed to the earliest Bornean export trade in forest products and in some cases still do so. Bezoar stones, concretions of tannins from the stomachs of leaf monkeys, have for long been one of the more bizarre items traded from the depths of the Borneo forests to the Chinese for medicinal uses. The horns of the hairy Asian Two-horned Rhinoceros were eagerly sought from early times. Despite the extreme rarity of this species now, and international campaigns and agreements forbidding commercial trade, horns and other parts of rhinoceroses still find their way from Borneo to China and other markets in South-east Asia. In 1990, research at the University of Hong Kong showed that, when imbibed, powdered rhino horn does indeed act to reduce fevers. However, so do the horns of other mammals, as well as aspirin and other synthetic chemicals. Unfortunately, while their horns are able to command prices in excess of US$50,000 per kilogram, it is not surprising that rhinoceroses are still under threat of extinction in their last scattered strongholds in the depths of the Bornean rainforests.

Although the distribution of elephants in Borneo is restricted to the extreme north-east, elephant ivory was also traded from Borneo at least two hundred years ago, as was another unusual form of ivory, the casque of the Helmeted Hornbill. Swiftlets, small birds which nest in caves, gave rise to yet another strange trade which is still in existence. The nests of some species are made from the birds' own saliva, which solidifies into hard filaments. The strange half-saucer shaped nests are harvested from fearsome dark cave walls and used to make birds' nest soup, a delicacy to the Chinese.

Perhaps least known but most fascinating of the early forest products traded from Borneo was wax from the nests of wild bees, used mainly for making candles. Almost all the bees' nests are made on the branches of Borneo's largest tree, the Mengaris. To reach them, collectors knock a series of sharpened bamboo pegs into the trunk, lashing them together with lianas to fashion a ladder. Traces of these ladders remain permanently in the tree trunk, in the form of calluses on the bark. In the 1820s, it was reported that about 150 tons of beeswax were obtained annually from the region of Kutai alone. This was taken down the Mahakam River by the collectors, and purchased by Bugis traders who transported it to Berau, where it was bought by traders from Sulu. From there it went to Manila, under Spanish rule, and to China. A local Dayak chief was reported to have nearly a thousand men employed solely in procuring beeswax from just one area north of Tenggarong.

Evidently many thousands of Bornean people were once involved in the beeswax industry, collecting the nests from many tens of thousands of trees. No wonder that a high proportion of old Mengaris trees all over Borneo bear scars of ladders made long ago. We can still marvel at the tenacity of the people who, generations ago, risked their lives by climbing high up massive trees, many days' hard travel from home. Accessible nests are still taken by people in rural areas to get the honey.

Sadly, monumental old Mengaris trees are now under threat from the chainsaw.

Until recently, few were felled, partly because of the traditional importance attached to them by rural folk, and partly because the wood is difficult to process. However, with a logging industry still geared to handling large logs which are becoming increasingly scarce and the frequent occurrence of Mengaris trees in accessible, lowland areas, we are likely to see a great many of these splendid giants cut down in the next few years.

A CHANGING WORLD

During the next century, most elements of Borneo's traditional economy will have altered radically or totally disappeared. The massive changes in society and land use that have been taking place over the last 30 years are continuing and are irreversible.

It is true that some aspects of the older way of life are being retained because people want them. All the Borneo governments are supporting the preservation of cultural traditions in one way or another. Sabah, Sarawak, Brunei and all the Kalimantan provinces have museums and other agencies which focus on local history and cultures, and all hold occasional or regular officially sponsored festivals, seminars and exhibitions.

In communities everywhere in Borneo, traditional clothes are donned and dances performed on special occasions. Longhouse lifestyles, the practice of communal rice planting, and time-honoured laws and penalties for crime, such as fines of pigs and buffaloes, are still widely retained. But all these are slowly being replaced as youngsters opt for alternatives. The special features of Bornean societies which foreign visitors come to see are getting harder to find. The young do not have body tattoos, stretched earlobes or traditional haircuts. Only a minority of individuals in a few communities now use blowpipes for hunting. Everyone, even in the remotest of communities, wears imported mass-produced clothing for routine activities, and those with money buy televisions, cassette recorders and the like. Most men wear a wrist-watch, even when performing traditional dances in traditional clothing. The skills of making artefacts such as metalware, hand-woven cloth, beadwork and

woodcarvings, even dug-out canoes are dying out.

The signs are that government support and the development of a significant tourism industry in Borneo may be needed to sustain many of the old skills. Bornean societies are attempting to keep alive regular use of their own language, but this is increasingly difficult with use of the national language (Malay or Indonesian) supplemented with English or Mandarin in schools.

COMMUNICATIONS

Air is nowadays the quickest and usual way to travel long distances in Borneo. There are frequent scheduled flights linking all the major towns and less frequent flights to some of the remoter communities. Commercial companies charter helicopters and small aeroplanes, and in some areas Christian mission programmes run aircraft. The permanent sealed road network is being steadily extended, mainly in the coastal zone, and public bus services are improving along with the roads. Separately, Sarawak and Sabah can be traversed by road from end to end. Only a gap at Brunei, expected to be filled by the end of this decade, prevents motorists from driving from Kuching to Tawau. Wherever there is logging, there are roads, which make previously remote communities suddenly very accessible. Some logging roads are eventually abandoned but, often, pioneering logging roads become the foundation – literally – of permanent government-maintained roads.

Despite the expanding road network, travel by boat retains its traditional importance, especially in Sarawak and Kalimantan, where there are regular public boat services on many of the larger rivers. Many families living on rivers or on the coast own a small boat powered by an outboard engine. In contrast, the public railway system, confined to western Sabah, has remained stagnant for several decades.

The use of telephones has increased greatly in recent years. In Sabah and Sarawak, the national telecommunications agency is installing solar-powered public telephones in many rural villages, while most companies that operate businesses out of town use mobile telephones.

THE OPENING UP OF FORESTS AND LAND

Petroleum, gas and coal resources were discovered in Borneo during the 19th century. During the present century Bornean petroleum and, more recently, gas have contributed very significantly to the economies of Indonesia, Malaysia and Brunei. These resources – found mainly in the coastal zone and offshore – are continuing to stimulate broader economic development in each of the three nations. A large share of the world's production of liquefied natural gas now comes from Borneo. Yet exploitation of these non-renewable natural resources has not had a major impact on land or forests.

The biggest impact of modern technology on Borneo came with the introduction in the 1950s of two basically simple kinds of machines – tractors with caterpillar-type tracks (bulldozers and tracked skidders)

plus the chainsaw. With these, roads can be made fairly rapidly on almost any kind of terrain, and massive trees can be felled and pulled to the road within an hour or two. The 1950s saw the beginning of an era where virtually no area in Borneo is off-limits to trade and industry. Since then, the development of roads has been a key factor changing the face of Borneo. This is not only because roads cause once inaccessible trees to become a valuable, easily available commodity, but also because they allow immigrant settlers, hunters and land speculators access to areas where previously people would never have gone or, at most, visited rarely on foot to seek small quantities of forest produce.

The process of logging in itself – which involves taking out some large trees and then abandoning the forest to regenerate naturally – is not a fundamental cause of either forest loss or social change in Borneo. Access provided by logging roads,

Chinese vendors at the railway halt near Papar, Sabah, in 1910. This railway line is still in operation and has daily public services.

however, plus large numbers of families each burning forest to make small temporary farms can lead to major forest loss, especially when fire is uncontrolled.

There is no clear-felling of forest as a method of harvesting timber in Borneo. Clear-felling costs energy and money and is done only where the people involved are going to plant crops. There are various circumstances under which this occurs. One is the case of groups of small-scale farmers mentioned above who, often taking advantage of logging roads, enter previously uninhabited land and open up farms. Typically, the farmers have the threefold aims of growing food, raising cash crops such as pepper, coffee, cocoa and rubber, and staking a claim to the land. This type of farming is often temporary or speculative, and with inadequate control of fire. Unfortunately, it is frequently labelled as shifting cultivation and thereby confused with traditional, stable hill rice farming systems.

Another circumstance where forest is lost is that of government-sponsored schemes, where large areas are cleared and planted with a few crops such as oil palm or rice. Infrastructure is developed through government grants and development bank loans, and large numbers of families are systematically resettled from overcrowded or poor areas elsewhere. A third case is that of companies which purchase land and plant crops for purely commercial reasons, typically employing immigrant labour to minimize costs and absenteeism. In combination, these are the main cause of forest loss in Borneo.

Logging, plantations, urbanization and industrialization have provided opportunities for people to earn money, which inevitably has contributed to the crumbling of the traditional economy. Money not only allows people to buy manufactured goods but also rice and other foods. With time, more and more people are preferring to abandon traditional occupations and buy what they would once have grown or acquired from the forest. This trend is reinforced by the great strides made by all the governments in Borneo in providing cheap or free education. More and more young people are seeking and receiving formal education to university level, in many cases overseas. Many Bornean families contain parents or grandparents who never went to school and who remain superbly capable of surviving by the traditional economy, living together with children or grandchildren who have spent their formative years in schools, proud of their rural roots but entirely at ease in a modern urban environment.

The old days of endless, unmapped forests are drawing to a close. New roads will continue to be built into previously remote areas. Plantations, along with new townships, industries, hydro-electric power facilities and so on, will continue to replace forest. Rough roads are gradually being gravelled and sealed. In the towns and coastal areas, planned industrial zones are appearing, as are international-class hotels. An urban middle class is emerging in the larger towns.

TOWNS AND CITIES

Superficially, most Bornean towns are rather alike in possessing a sprawl of uninteresting low-rise buildings, both residential and commercial, with daytime traffic jams in the centre, relieved by a good scattering of trees. A closer look reveals more of the history of the locality and the characteristics of the people. Banjarmasin and Bandar Seri Begawan are alike in having a long history, with their origins dating back at least 600 years as pre-Islamic kingdoms, which later became regional centres of Muslim influence and trade. Both retain a strongly Malay character and both have extensive townships built over water. Pontianak and Samarinda were founded as towns by Muslim immigrants in the 18th century, while Palangkaraya is a small administrative centre.

With beginnings in the mid-19th century, Kuching is one of the most pleasant towns in Borneo, containing interesting buildings dating from the Rajah Brooke era, now interspersed with tall modern buildings including some splendid hotels. Kota Kinabalu (formerly Jesselton) and Sandakan were founded under the rule of the British North Borneo Company and both were razed at the end of World War Two. The present towns are almost entirely new. Kota Kinabalu has several attractive modern buildings, including the 28-storey Sabah Foundation Building which houses one of Borneo's best libraries.

TOURISM AND ECOTOURISM

Until very recently, few tourists visited any part of Borneo. Now, Borneo is becoming an increasingly popular destination for travellers, especially those interested in nature and conservation. Several offshore islands provide some of the finest coral reef diving in the world while, inland, international interest in the tropical rainforests has made Borneo a prime choice for people wanting to experience first-hand this hitherto largely unknown land.

Some idea of the rate of development and effects of ecotourism may be gained from examples in Sabah, where there is a diverse array of accessible natural features within a relatively small area. Following the first ascent of Gunung Kinabalu by Hugh Low in 1851, there were 53 recorded visits to the mountain during the next century. Now, about 200,000 people visit the mountain and 10 per cent climb to the top annually, all taking the same route. Yet the environmental effects are trivial. The mountain retains its magic and all its wild species.

A large proportion of income from tourists goes, directly or indirectly, to members of local communities. Until the mid-1980s, virtually the only people to visit 11 hectare (27 acre) Pulau Sipadan were collectors of turtle eggs, who had been given customary rights to do so by the British administration in 1916. 'Discovered' by a dive tour operator as one of the world's prime coral reef dive sites, Sipadan is now visited daily by dozens of divers. With the advent of dive tours, interest in the turtles grew, and it became apparent that decades of egg collection was threatening their survival. In 1993, under the supervision of the Sabah government, the three tour operators on Sipadan signed an agreement with the traditional turtle egg collectors to buy out the rights to all eggs for an annual sum of 50,000 Malaysian ringgit. All eggs are now left to hatch naturally on the beach of Sipadan. The island is the subject of a territorial dispute between Indonesia and Malaysia but on-going friendly discussions are likely to resolve this in the near future.

In 1989, a study conducted by World Wide Fund For Nature (WWF) Malaysia for the Sabah Ministry of Tourism and Environmental Development showed that the forests of the lower Kinabatangan River were one of the prime wildlife areas in Malaysia, with tremendous potential for ecotourism but under threat of total destruction through conversion to agriculture. At that time, a dozen or so tourists visited the area annually. In 1993, over 2,000 tourists visited Kinabatangan and the government is finalizing plans for a new wildlife sanctuary which will protect rare species such as the Proboscis Monkey and Oriental Darter. So far, ecotourism is supporting conservation efforts in Sabah. One of the constraints to a similar situation elsewhere in Borneo is relative difficulty of access and paucity of accommodation out of town.

There are signs that tourism may be able to help sustain dying crafts and cultures, especially in Sarawak and Kalimantan, where several of the ethnic groups are particularly rich in these aspects. There is always the risk that cultures will thus become totally commercialized and lose their meaning to the indigenous people themselves. So far this has not happened and most local observers remain optimistic that tourism can support the cultural traditions of Borneo.

CONSERVATION

Conservation anywhere involves wise management of all natural resources, especially land, soil, water, vegetation and wildlife, and also an understanding of the needs of people caught between loyalty to an old way of life and the pressures of the new. In Borneo, most of the land is naturally covered in forest and its management is the key to protection of the whole environment from loss and pollution that in turn will affect the human population. The economic developments that are sweeping through Borneo make it vitally important that the island's most outstanding and potentially valuable resource – the enormous wealth of biological diversity contained in its forests – is conserved for future generations.

PROTECTING FOREST LANDS

In Borneo, as elsewhere, the future of land and forest remains uncertain as long as their ownership is in doubt. Without secure tenure, both resources effectively remain up for grabs, and no one has any incentive to ensure sustainable use – even if both are legally government property. Two prerequisites for wise management of any forest land and biological diversity, therefore, are that both long-term ownership of the land and rights to manage the forest on it must be clearly agreed upon and specifically guaranteed by law.

In the past, there was little real human pressure on Borneo's land and forests, except in a few small areas. The concepts of ownership and rights in forest land were essential ingredients to the functioning of Bornean communities, but they did not involve written documentation and seldom was there conflict with other claimants. There was barely any connection with a world economy – which is nowadays pumping in cash in return for timber and plantation products. While traditional communities do still depend on the forests and remain custodians of a vast repository of knowledge about wild species, it is no longer realistic to assume that rural communities acting alone will be able to implement conservation measures.

The simplest and ultimately cheapest basis for the goal of wise forest management is for governments, with specialist advice, to identify which land should ideally remain under forest cover, and undisturbed, for conservation purposes, and which may be managed for wood production. In addition, areas may be designated for traditional harvesting and hunting by rural communities. All this land should then be constituted by law as 'permanent forest estate', never to be released for other purposes. This process is difficult to achieve and does not guarantee success. Yet without it, all other conservation efforts will be expensive, protracted and mostly doomed to ultimate failure.

In the world context, the Borneo situation gives grounds for a fair degree of optimism. For a start, more than half the island still retains forest cover, albeit now heavily disturbed in most areas. Importantly, much of this forest is under government control, being either already reserved as forest reserves, parks or sanctuaries, or available for reservation, or held under native customary tenure. This means that the Borneo governments, unlike many others elsewhere, are not in a position of having to buy back vast land areas from private owners at enormous cost or to pay landowners annually to retain forest. There is still breathing-space to get more forest land reserved in a permanent forest estate, for strict conservation, for sustainable timber production and for traditional community use. Fortunately, all the Borneo governments seem to be working towards this goal. Sabah has taken the lead, having estab-

lished about half of its land area as permanent forest estate by 1984.

It is important to appreciate that areas to be preserved undisturbed (collectively called 'protection forests') and areas to be used for timber production (collectively called 'production forests') both have vital roles to play in conservation. Many species and ecological linkages between plants and animals depend on the existence of protection forests. Some conservationists focus entirely on these, however, not realizing that production forests cover a very much larger land area and that one round of logging rarely results in the loss of more than half of the vegetation cover.

Historically, permanent forest estates have been generated in piecemeal fashion and none of the Bornean regions is now likely to end up with the conservationist's ideal. In general, what happened was that a few rather small areas of outstanding natural scenery were designated for protection many years ago. Later, much larger areas of lowland forest were designated for timber production. Since then, however, starting in the 1970s, extensive areas of production forests have been redesignated for conversion to permanent agriculture, leaving mainly hill ranges and mountains both for timber production and for environmental protection purposes.

From the 1960s, a variety of agencies including in-country government departments, United Nations and foreign aid agencies, universities and non-governmental organizations have been involved in building up the permanent forest estate in all the Bornean nations. The World Wide Fund For Nature, for example, has been active since the 1970s in assisting governments in Sabah, Sarawak and Kalimantan to identify and conduct research and surveys in areas important for conservation.

There are now many existing and proposed protected areas in Borneo, all of which are important for conservation. In Sabah, Mount Kinabalu has been described by one eminent botanist as possessing 'the richest and most remarkable assemblage of plants in the world'. Danum Valley contains a wide variety of dipterocarp forest habitats and their fauna, including rhinoceroses and elephants, plus an active Field Studies Centre for research and education. Sabah has three parks which are unusual in incorporating marine and island habitats: Tunku Abdul Rahman, Turtle Islands and Pulau Tiga. The proposed Kinabatangan Wildlife Sanctuary includes highly endangered floodplain forest habitats and natural lakes.

In Sarawak, Gunung Mulu National Park is famous for its fantastic limestone caves, while the readily accessible Lambir Hills National Park is renowned among botanists for possessing an enormous diversity of rare trees in one small area. Lanjak-Entimau Wildlife Sanctuary and the adjacent Batang Ai National Park represent the largest protected areas in Sarawak. In Brunei Darussalam, the rugged Batu Apoi Forest Reserve incorporates the Kuala Belalong Field Studies Centre run by Universiti Brunei Darussalam.

Gunung Palung Nature Reserve in West Kalimantan contains an interesting spectrum of forest types from the coast to mountain peaks. In Central Kalimantan, the Tanjung Puting National Park consists of examples of coastal lowland forests and is a stronghold for Orang-utans, while Bukit Raya in the interior supports a large area of remote, biologically rich forests. The massive Kayan-Mentarang Nature Reserve in northern East Kalimantan is Borneo's largest protected area and research being conducted there is unusual in integrating anthropology and biology.

LOOKING AHEAD

Planning for conservation in Borneo is no easy task. The most serious considerations fall into four main groupings. First, because agriculture yields more product per hectare and hence greater immediate profits than forests, there is a continuing pressure to convert forests to permanent agriculture. Most of the fertile lowlands of Borneo have either been converted or, under present plans, are available for conversion to permanent agriculture including such crops as oil palm, cocoa, pepper, rubber and rice.

The conversion of the bulk of the lowland forests makes much sense in conventional economic terms and is probably inevitable. Yet the trend has some profound implications, as yet perhaps unrealized. One aspect is that most of the production forests in Borneo are now situated in hill

ranges where growth of new wood is very slow, because the best lands for wood production have been allocated instead for agriculture. This means that, while much money has been invested in planting crops which require a constant cheap labour supply, the capacity to produce tropical hardwoods for free by natural regeneration has been drastically reduced. Another aspect is that logging in hill land leads to more erosion and sedimentation of water supplies than logging in the lowlands.

There are also implications for wildlife. Some species need lowland forests to survive in the long term as wild breeding populations. The Orang-utan, a species which in Borneo is concentrated mainly in forests below 150 metres (500 feet) altitude, is an example. During the past two decades, the natural habitat of several thousands of Bornean Orang-utans has been converted to planned agricultural schemes and plantations. Some of these apes have been taken to 'rehabilitation centres' in protected forests and some may have moved into adjacent areas. Others, however, will have either died or been exported illegally to destinations overseas. Many conservation organizations and dedicated individuals have spent time and money seeking ways to handle their plight, yet the situation is at root a symptom of more or less planned and inevitable forest loss rather than a direct cause of the endangered status of the species. Instead of focusing on individual animals, conservation effort would be more usefully devoted to ensuring the establishment of a permanent forest estate which includes adequate samples of all forest types, and not merely land unsuitable for agriculture.

The second major problem is that in most regions of Borneo except Brunei, the annual extraction of timber has for many years exceeded – in some areas by five-fold – the rate at which wood is being produced by natural regeneration. Yet in all these regions, and not even counting unprocessed log exports, the local wood-based industry alone is now geared to needing more wood than can be supplied by the natural Bornean forests. The implications are that Borneo's wood-based industry will shift from use of massive trees to much smaller ones, of which there are countless millions

still in the natural forests and which can also be grown in much shorter periods.

Here there are two important conservation implications. One is that logging intensity is likely to increase in natural forests, and many trees crucial to conserving biological diversity will in the future be taken. The other is that tree plantations, which can produce wood at rates at least ten times higher than in the natural forests, will be needed as part of a strategy to relieve logging pressure on the natural forests. Unfortunately, the economics of tree plantations are such that only governments and very large corporations have the resources to develop them. At present, tree plantations for wood production cover only about 0.1 per cent of Borneo's land area and, even if investment does come about, it will take several decades before they are capable of supporting a major industry.

The coming decade is likely to see intensified cutting of both smaller trees and defective large trees in the natural forests. For conservation, intensified cutting is a major concern. Unfortunately, the few existing studies on the biological effects of logging in Borneo have been done after only one round of logging in old growth forests, and on ecologically robust species such as mammals and birds. Without further scientific studies and appropriate modifications in forest management, Borneo's biological diversity is increasingly under threat from logging as well as forest clearance. Organisms sensitive to small changes in humidity and light, such as frogs or orchids, are likely to suffer most. Hornbills and other species which require nesting holes are likely to disappear outside protection forests as defective trees, formerly left untouched, are felled to supply local mills.

The third consideration for conservationists to face is that, with a human population which is expanding rapidly both in size and distribution, and with a growing network of roads, it is increasingly difficult to moderate trends which have been set in motion. For example, available data suggest that possibly over half a million hectares of forest were lost annually in Borneo during the 1980s. If correct, this means that about 7 per cent of Borneo's land area was deforested in a single decade.

Once widespread but increasingly rare

habitats like lowland dipterocarp forests and riverine forests are especially difficult to protect when fragmented and surrounded by settlements and plantations. Whereas in the past, people cleared, farmed and settled mostly on fertile lands, they are now pushing into land which is unsuitable for swidden farming and which cannot sustain permanent agriculture in the absence of impractically high levels of fertilizer and management. Under this type of threat are the heath forests, which occur on flat land superficially attractive for settlement but actually unsuitable for any form of agriculture. In the past, no one would have contemplated settling on heath land.

With the waning of times when land settlement was primarily a means of establishing a community and growing rice, and the passage to a society where land is essentially a cash-generating exchangeable commodity, accessible forest land is increasingly viewed as a place to enter, clear and establish ownership claims. The short-term solution is to identify critically endangered sites and to seek case-by-case protective measures. The only realistic long-term remedy, however, is to provide all Borneans with adequate education – not on the beauty of nature and a clean environment – but sufficient so that they are able to make a living in the modern, mainly industrialized economy and are not forced to survive as small-scale rural farmers.

Forest fires are arguably the most serious of all threats to conservation. Prior to 1982, no one really believed that fire could wipe out Bornean forests on any significant scale, but fires which raged in northern and eastern Borneo during a drought which lasted from September 1982 until June 1983 destroyed or seriously damaged over 4 million hectares (10 million acres) of forest. Subsequent study revealed that the fires were concentrated in regions containing logged forests and rural subsistence farmers. The same parts of Borneo have experienced several shorter dry spells since 1983 which have been associated with less extensive forest fires. It is now clear that old growth forest is not immune from fire, but that the abundance of dead wood coupled with the accessibility provided by roads makes logged forests and settlers in previously remote areas a highly risky combination during long dry spells. One carelessly set fire can wipe out millions of dollars' worth of timber and lead to the extinction of localized rare plant species, yet there is no sure way of prevention.

MOVES IN THE RIGHT DIRECTION

Reduced emphasis on agricultural expansion will be necessary if Borneo's forests and biological diversity are to be conserved.

While economic diversification and industrialization are needed to improve individual human opportunities and help relieve the long-term pressures on forests and land, there are reasons to believe that forest-based industries should ideally continue to form the economic backbone of Borneo as a whole. The vast land area and climatic conditions are suitable for production of large quantities of wood. Many existing communities are familiar with and geared to forestry in one way or another. The tourism industry is expanding rapidly in some parts of Borneo, and the sites of greatest interest to most tourists are forests.

There is scope for considerable innovation in forestry and many interesting projects with potential for expansion have already been quietly introduced in Borneo. In Kalimantan, some rural farmers have for long been planting rattan in their farms. In Sabah, both the government and private sector have developed large scale rattan plantations in logged forests, with promising results. Rattan is an excellent crop all round, because its cultivation requires trees and therefore provides inbuilt incentives to retain and manage forest. An innovation introduced by Sabah Forest Industries to supply its paper mill is the provision of tree seedlings to traditional farmers, who plant them out in hill rice fields. When the time comes to plant the fallow land with rice again years later, the fields will be full of trees that can be sold to the mill.

Tree plantations are still highly traditional in using monocultures of introduced species, but there are signs of interest in use of mixtures of native trees. In East Kalimantan, the Wanariset-Samboja research station is experimenting in practical ways of propogating dipterocarp trees on degraded land in collaboration with the timber industry, smallholders and shifting cultivators. In the Ulu Segama area of Sabah, near to Danum Valley, the Sabah Foundation has struck agreements with Dutch and American organizations for funds to enrich logged forests with native trees and to carry out logging methods which minimize damage to the forest. Both projects are aimed at finding ways to enhance tropical production forest management and at the same time help stabilize the global carbon dioxide balance.

At present, it is often not clear whether a particular area will remain under forest, and if not, what it will be converted to and who will own and manage it. More detailed planning of land use and land tenure on a regional scale plus rapid implementation of those plans is becoming imperative for both economic improvement and environmental management. Yet in Borneo, as elsewhere, big plans alone are insufficient. Some of the best achievements in conservation-based development are coming about through the *ad hoc* efforts of non-governmental organizations and the corporate sector.

BORNEO'S FUTURE

For Borneo there is no turning back. The land that once seemed to exist only in the tall tales of the old travellers is now well and truly in the 20th century and playing an important role in world commerce and economics. More and more people are seizing the opportunity to see for themselves the natural wonders that make this one of the most beautiful places on earth. Nothing can stop the tide of progress but with it are brought education, a higher standard of living and an awareness of the need to protect and conserve all that was once taken for granted. The signs surely augur well for the future.

THE LAND

V ast, rugged, equatorial and wet, Borneo is an island clothed in tropical rainforests. Plants and fungi thrive in its ideal combination of warmth, a lack of
distinct seasons, abundant water and light. Yet the form and fertility of the
land vary widely from place to place. Together, these factors have permitted the
evolution of a great diversity of species. Every site has its own particular kind of
forest and array of plants.

The coastline is fringed with muddy mangroves, Nipa palm swamps and sandy
beaches. Inland are peat swamps, meandering rivers mighty and small, and
plains, some rich and lush, others sandy and infertile. Outcrops of hard rocks,
such as limestone, dot the landscape. Progressing further inland, rolling hills give
way to steeper slopes and dramatic valleys. Here, the natural landscape is typically one of timber-rich forests, in which trees with huge, buttressed trunks soar
up through the dim green shade under the canopy of leaves. A feature of many of
the forests is an abundance of climbing plants which use the trees as support.
Higher still are mountain forests, of lower stature, containing oaks, laurels and
conifers, typically mossy, sometimes rich in orchids, pitcher plants and rhododendrons, and often wreathed in clouds. On mountain tops, the plants are short and
gnarled. Gunung Kinabalu in Sabah is the highest mountain in South-east Asia.

Apart from its timber, mainland Borneo contains many natural riches like gold,
diamonds, coal, petroleum and natural gas. Less readily definable in monetary
terms, and barely utilised, is its wealth of plants other than timber trees.
Countless species, many still undescribed, are potentially valuable in cultivation,
above all perhaps as sources of medicine. This grand and predominantly green
island, though its huge scale is breathtaking, is at the same time intricate, subtle
and enormously complex in its detail.

At Bako National Park, Sarawak, sandstone cliffs (left) and freshwater streams (above) demonstrate the intricate beauty of nature in Borneo.

PREVIOUS PAGES
Page 58: *The Borneo landscape is richly varied. The Sarawak coastline near Santubong (above left) and the islands off Semporna in eastern Sabah (above right) exemplify the sandy beaches which fringe much of the coastline and many offshore islands. Inland, rugged hill ranges, which typically receive over 3,000 millimetres (110 inches) of rainfall annually, support forests of fantastic biological diversity, like the catchment of the Temburong River in Brunei (below left). Between the hilly interior and the coastline are numerous rivers and swampy floodplains, like the Sekunir River floodplain at Tanjung Puting National Park in Central Kalimantan (below right).*

Page 59: Globba atrosanguinea, *one of many wild gingers in the Borneo rainforest.*

Below: *A palm,* Pholidocarpus maiadum, *is one of many beautiful plants at Bako, Sarawak. The luxuriant growth of the rainforest appears to belie the fact that much of the land consists of infertile, sandy soils. The plants rely on the rapid decomposition of forest debris for their nutrients.*

Opposite: *Coastal scene at Santubong, Sarawak. Nipa palms line the right-hand bank of the stream. This palm was once an important source of thatch and sugar for coastal communities in Borneo.*

Natural forests on the sandy coastal plains of western and southern Borneo are of low stature, containing many pole-sized trees. In these forests, known as heath forests, mutually beneficial relationships between plants and ants have evolved. Growing on the branches of trees, the thick, waxy leaves of Dischidia nummularia (left) *form shelters for ants. In return, the ants bring in food such as insects, whose bodies are trapped and provide scarce nutrients to the plant. A variety of taller forests can also be found in these regions of Borneo. Examples may be seen in Samunsam Wildlife Sanctuary* (below left) *and from the lower Rajang River* (below right).

Dipterocarp forests are among the most spectacular of the lowland forests in Borneo, in terms of their stature and diversity of plant and animal species. Most of the large trees in these forests belong to a single family, the Dipterocarpaceae, of which there are nearly 300 species. They are the main timber trees of Borneo. Many large trees develop huge supporting buttresses, such as these in Sarawak's Niah National Park (above).

The limestone outcrops at Niah (left) contain caves inhabited by prehistoric people over many thousands of years, which represent the most important archaeological site in Borneo. The view from inside the Great Cave at Niah (opposite) is probably much as it would have appeared to Borneo's earliest human inhabitants. Dipterocarp forest cloaks the flat land while a different flora covers the limestone cliffs.

Sarawak's Lambir Hills National Park contains an exceptional variety of tree species. The Lambir Hills forest also has many lianas – woody climbing plants which use trees for support as they grow – like this Bauhinia kockiana (above). *Scenic and accessible by road, the Park is not only important for the conservation of biological diversity, but also has a great amenity and recreational value.*

Left: *Waterfall at Lambir Hills. Attractive palms and shrubs drape the steep sandstone valley, kept luxuriant by constant dampness and warmth.*

Below: *A profile of the forest at Lambir Hills. Superficially similar, each tree is of a different species. Some are adapted to conditions of low light intensity, and remain small, while others grow constantly, eventually emerging above the general forest canopy.*

Above: *The Tutoh River, which provides access to Gunung Mulu National Park in Sarawak. In the distance Gunung Mulu itself rises to a height of 2,376 metres (7,795 feet) above sea level. The Park contains river valleys and plains which rise steadily to a line of steep rugged limestone mountains and deep gorges. This varied geology and topography has resulted in the evolution of a variety of natural habitats. Rainfall here is some of the heaviest in Borneo, ranging from about 5,000 to 7,000 millimetres (200 to 275 inches) per year, and eventually draining into the Baram River* (right). *Together, rain and time have acted on the limestone to produce one of the most spectacular cave systems in the world. Deer Cave* (below) *is the world's largest cave passage, while the 300 metre (990 feet) high Sarawak Chamber is the world's largest cave chamber.*

Rhododendrons are an attractive group of plants, with showy flowers, sometimes beautifully scented, and are of considerable horticultural value. Some species are represented by different varieties, with differently coloured flowers. Hybrids between two species are commonly found in the wild. In Borneo, rhododendrons grow only on wet, infertile acidic soils and peat, or as epiphytes (that is, on the stems and branches of other plants). Their roots form associations with special fungi known as mycorrhizae, which assist the rhododendrons to obtain scarce nutrients.

Above left: Rhododendron acuminatum, a species confined to ridges between 2,800 and 3,400 metres (9,200 and 11,200 feet) on Gunung Kinabalu. Blooming mainly from February to April, its flowers are pollinated by birds.

Centre: Rhododendron durionifolium, a species widespread in the mountain forests of Borneo at altitudes of between 1,400 and 1,800 metres (4,600 and 5,900 feet).

Below left: The flowers of Rhododendron suaveolens, another species of the middle range of mountain forests, have a spicy jasmine-like scent.

Below right: Rhododendron fallacinum, a species found in the mountains of western Sabah between 1,200 and 2,500 metres (3,900 and 8,200 feet).

Insectivorous pitcher plants (Nepenthes species) have leaves modified to form traps. Insects, attracted by a glandular secretion on the rim of the pitcher, slide down the slippery walls into water containing a digestive enzyme where they are absorbed. Bornean species include Nepenthes stenophylla (above left) *and* Nepenthes villosa (above right).

Fungi play a vital role in the forests of Borneo in breaking down dead plant material and releasing nutrients into the forest system. Many fungi add splashes of colour to the dark forest interior, including this cup fungus (Cookeina species) (right), the delicate Mycena *species (below right) and the evil-smelling Maiden's Veil,* Dictyophora duplicata (below).

Rugged hill ranges, cloaked in tall dipterocarp forests and dissected by networks of rivers and streams, characterize the interior of Borneo. Across most of the island, these forests have been or are being opened up for their enormous timber resources. In Brunei, however, the wealth generated from petroleum has meant that there is little pressure to log the forests. The forests of the upper Temburong River (left) are totally protected and a field studies centre has been established at Kuala Belalong. The splendour and variety of plants inside the dipterocarp forests of Borneo are revealed by looking at the forest from different angles (above and right).

Above: *The Kuala Belalong Field Studies Centre, set up in early 1991, quickly established its international credentials as the headquarters of a 15-month joint Universiti Brunei Darussalam/Royal Geographical Society expedition. Some 50 scientists from eight countries took part in more than 33 short projects and nine long-term core studies designed to gather background data for the development of the centre as a research facility. The projects included studies of ants, termites, woodlice, beetles, frogs, birds, bats, ferns and rattans. At the end of the expedition, the centre was opened to other visitors.*

Left: *In their quest for light, woody lianas grow upwards, using trees for support, and twine throughout the forest canopy. These lianas add to the diversity of forest life, providing food, pathways and ecological niches for animals.*

Opposite: *A small tributary of the Temburong River. Countless streams like this drain the island of Borneo, providing clean drinking water for animal life and, in many cases, for human communities. Outside urban areas, most communities throughout Borneo rely to some extent on streams or rivers for their domestic water requirements. In some areas, small forest streams are dammed to supply constant clean water, through a pipe and by the action of gravity, to villages downstream.*

PREVIOUS PAGES
A view from the top of Bukit Belalong, Brunei, of inland Borneo, its thickly forested mountains wreathed in cloud.

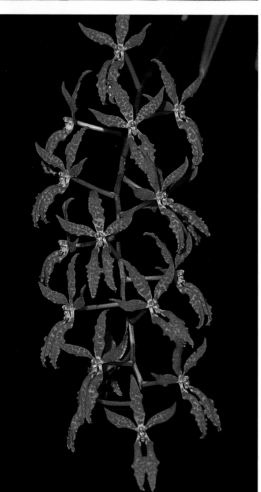

Of all the families of plants in Borneo, the orchids have the greatest number of species – perhaps 3,000 or so in all. The flowers of most are small and inconspicuous, but some are spectacularly beautiful.

Above left: *First collected by John Whitehead, the earliest zoologist on Gunung Kinabalu,* Paphiopedilum rothschildianum *is an extremely rare and handsome slipper orchid, still known only from two sites in the foothills of the mountain.*

Above: Vanda dearei, *an epiphytic orchid with horticultural value, once widespread along the banks of larger rivers in Borneo, has been much depleted by forest clearance and collectors.*

Below left: Renathera bella, *a beautiful orchid with great potential for breeding for the cut-flower market, is confined to a few sites of ultrabasic soils (those rich in heavy metals) in Sabah.*

OPPOSITE PAGE
Above left: Phalaenopsis pantherina, *with its showy, long-lasting flowers, is widespread in Borneo, but it does not occur in any protected areas and is considered to be in danger of extinction.*

Centre left: Trichoglottis smithii, *another endangered orchid, known only from Sabah.*

Above right: Vanda hookeriana, *a species of peat swamps, near the Sekunir River, Tanjung Puting National Park, Kalimantan.*

Below left: Bulbophyllum uniflorum, *a member of the largest genus of orchids in Borneo, occurs in shaded sites in the forests of western Borneo.*

Centre and bottom right: *The remarkable* Dimorphorchis lowii, *which bears two differently coloured flowers on a single plant.*

Opposite: *Gunung Kinabalu (4,101 metres; 13,455 feet) is the highest mountain not only in Borneo but in the entire South-east Asian region. Its lofty, jagged peaks can be seen on clear days from most parts of northern Sabah. The middle levels of Gunung Kinabalu are covered in montane forests (above), moderate in stature and quite different from the dipterocarp forests lower down. Trees of the oak, myrtle, laurel and conifer families are common here.*

Right: *A clear trail is maintained up Gunung Kinabalu, allowing nearly 20,000 visitors annually to climb to the mountain's peak.*

Gunung Kinabalu supports a rich variety of plant life, possibly the most diverse on earth for such a small area. The montane vegetation, above about 1,500 metres (5,000 feet), contains strictly tropical forms of plants as well as a wide range of species closely related to plants known from temperate regions, including Taiwan, southern Japan, China and New Zealand. As well as trees of the families mentioned on page 79, for example, there are also trees and shrubs of the magnolia, anise and witch hazel families, and endemic raspberries and buttercups.

Top left: Schefflera *species, a small tree near the Kinabalu Park headquarters. The roots and leaves are used medicinally by some rural communities.*

Top right: *The attractive, ripening fruits of a* Clerodendrum *species (1,500 metres; 5,000 feet).*

Centre: *The Kinabalu balsam,* Impatiens platyphylla, *a herb which occurs in damp, rocky sites on Gunung Kinabalu.*

Bottom left: Vaccinium stapfianum, *a compact, bushy plant whose young leaves are red in colour (3,300 metres; 11,000 feet).*

Bottom right: Schima breviforma, *a shrub which belongs to the tea family (3,700 metres; 12,000 feet). The snowy white flowers offset the sombre leaves of this plant.*

A view to the peaks of Gunung Kinabalu (above) from the upper montane vegetation zone at Panar Laban (3,300 metres; 11,000 feet). The summit zone consists of bare granite, pushed upwards from under the earth's surface less than a million years ago. Thousands of feet of overlying sand and mudstone were eroded away. During the last ice age, the summit was covered with ice, which melted less than 10,000 years ago. Boulders and grooves, gouged by moving rocks embedded between the mountain top and the ice, can still be seen today on the summit plateau (right).

The Crocker Range forms the mountainous backbone of western Sabah, with ridgetops ranging from 900 to nearly 1,500 metres (3,000 to 5,000 feet) above sea level (left). Established as a National Park in 1984, the Crocker Range represents a crucial water catchment area for the rice-growing communities in the surrounding plains and valleys. The south end of the Crocker Range is cut through by the Padas River (below), which forms a gorge. In the early 1900s, the British North Borneo Company built a railway along the side of the Padas Gorge. Still in operation, the railway links the towns of Tenom, Beaufort and Kota Kinabalu.

Opposite: Beautiful Pulau Tiga (meaning 'Three Island') lies off the west coast of Sabah. The name refers to the form of the island, which consists of three low peaks. With white, coral-sand beaches and entirely cloaked in natural forest, Pulau Tiga was reserved in 1978 as a Park, along with two smaller islands.

Originally established in the 1930s for the supply of timber for local use, Sepilok Forest Reserve, outside Sandakan in eastern Sabah, was given totally protected status in 1957. Sepilok now preserves examples of the natural dipterocarp forests (above) which have otherwise mostly disappeared from the Sandakan area. The Reserve also contains examples of heath forests. Amongst the variety of plants which occur in Sepilok are climbing figs (left). The attractive fruits, the size of an orange, are actually hard, astringent and full of latex.

The coastal zone of eastern Borneo differs from that in the west. In the east, the mangrove forests are more extensive. Mangrove forests, which develop on mudflats subject to frequent inundation by the sea, represent important feeding and shelter zones for a variety of marine life including fish, molluscs and prawns. In the past, mangrove trees were important sources of charcoal and tannin (for tanning leather and ropes); mangrove poles are still used for piling. Inland from the mangrove, eastern Borneo has extensive areas of freshwater swamps interspersed with fertile, rolling lowlands – unlike the infertile sandy plains and peat swamps of western Borneo.

Right: Segaliud River, Sabah. The riverside vegetation includes Nipa palms and old orchards of durians.

Below: A channel through mangrove forest at the mouth of the Labuk River, Sabah.

The dipterocarp forests of north-eastern Borneo are amongst the grandest on the entire island. They contain extensive stands of large trees, many greater than 50 metres (160 feet) in height, and an undergrowth packed with a diversity of small trees, lianas, palms, shrubs and herbs. The forests are rich in wildlife including monkeys, apes, wild cats, bears, elephants, hornbills and pheasants. Examples of these forests, both logged for timber and in their original condition, can be seen in the Ulu Segama Forest Reserve in eastern Sabah.

Above: Hill dipterocarp forest, viewed from a roadside in Ulu Segama Forest Reserve. Pioneering experiments in reduced impact logging techniques and planting seedlings of timber trees are being conducted in this extensive region of geologically complex hill ranges. Nearby, Gunung Silam, a compact coastal mountain of ultrabasic rock at the logging road entrance, is regarded by botanists as one of Sabah's most interesting natural habitats.

Left: Lowland dipterocarp forest on the banks of the Segama River in Danum Valley Conservation Area, a section of the Ulu Segama Forest Reserve. Danum Valley has a well established field studies centre, where many biological studies have been conducted to compare old growth and logged dipterocarp forests.

The islands off north-eastern Borneo are not only beautiful, but also important for the survival of a number of rare and unusual wildlife species. These include marine turtles, which lay their eggs on the sandy beaches, and a bizarre Megapode bird, the Dusky Scrubfowl (Megapodius freycinet). The coral reefs which have developed around these islands are, likewise, both beautiful and the sustenance for many marine creatures.
Above: Pulau Sipadan, a world-famous diving site, which rises from a depth of about 600 metres (2,000 feet). Its coral reef is clearly visible. Right: Islands in Darvel Bay, viewed from the foot of Gunung Silam in Sabah. This group of islands includes ultrabasic rocks, the peaks of extinct volcanos, and ancient exposed coral reefs.

FOLLOWING PAGES
A tropical white-sand beach on one of the Semporna islands off Sabah.

The variety of herbs, shrubs and small woody plants in Borneo is often overlooked because of the prominence of the trees. Although often inconspicuous, the flowers and fruits of many species reveal great beauty when seen at close range.

Above: Mussaenda frondosa *near Bario, northern Sarawak. The small, delicate flowers are fragrant and were formerly made into scent in some areas, while the large whitish calyx lobe can be eaten as a vegetable, and the leaves may be used medicinally.*

Centre left: Costus speciosus, *a member of the ginger family, at Niah National Park, Sarawak. The fleshy rhizomes of this species are edible and useful when other food is scarce. They are believed to possess medicinal properties.*

Below left: Baccaurea *species, a small tree with sour fruits, at Ulu Segama Forest Reserve, Sabah.*

OPPOSITE PAGE
Above: Dianella ensifolia, *a herb whose fruits, roots and leaves are sometimes used in traditional medicines.*

Below left: Dillenia *species, a riverside bush, on the Menanggul tributary of the Kinabatangan River, Sabah.*

Below right: Begonia *species, one of many little-known forest herbs with horticultural potential, in Ulu Segama Forest Reserve, Sabah.*

Above: *Pulau Sangalakki, off East Kalimantan, a beautiful small island fringed with palms and white-sand beaches. The coral reef around its shore makes it an increasingly popular location for divers.*

Above: *The bank of the Sangatta River near Kutai National Park, East Kalimantan. The trees are a species of the mango genus,* Mangifera caesia, *known locally by various names including Belunu, Bundu and Wanyi. Occurring in the wild in Borneo but often found in old orchards, their presence at the site depicted here probably indicates a long-abandoned village. The fruits have a remarkable and unique aromatic, creamy and somewhat bitter flavour.*

Left: *Mangrove trees (Rhizophora species) at low tide near Kutai National Park. The small size and spacing of the trees indicate that the forest at this site is quite heavily harvested but capable of regenerating itself naturally.*

Opposite: *Lowland dipterocarp forest between Samarinda and Bontang, East Kalimantan. The ragged silhouette of the forest indicates that it has been logged. If protected from fire, repeated logging and clearance by farmers, forest such as this will regenerate naturally through growth of seedlings and young trees.*

Above: *Drowned trees in Semayang Lake off the Mahakam River, East Kalimantan. Freshwater lakes such as this provide abundant fish, which are consumed by both people and wildlife.*

Left: *The village of Longnawan in the upper Kayan River valley, East Kalimantan. Inland communities like this were traditionally self-sufficient for most of their needs, especially food. Hill rice and wet rice are staple crops. Most of the trees in this landscape bear edible fruits or other useful products such as sticky latex (spread on suitable surfaces to trap birds by their feet), bark (for making baskets and temporary walls) and medicines.*

Borneo is rich in wild gingers. About 170 species have been described and more remain to be discovered. Gingers offer great potential for the discovery of medicinal substances and flavourings, and as ornamental plants. The flowers of wild gingers are typically reddish in colour and fleshy, but there is great variety in their form and size. Above: Hedychium muluensis *of northern Sarawak.* Above centre: Zingiber *species near Bario, Sarawak.* Above right: *An undescribed ginger at Kutai National Park, East Kalimantan.*

The bizarre Rafflesia *flower, which can sometimes reach nearly a metre (3 feet) in diameter, is a parasite which can bloom only on the roots and stems of a wild vine,* Tetrastigma, *and has no stem, root or leaves of its own.* Centre right: Rafflesia pricei *in its natural habitat with host vine in Sabah's Rafflesia Virgin Jungle Reserve.* Below right: Rafflesia tuan-mudae. *Below:* Rafflesia tengku-adlinii, *discovered in 1988.*

Left and opposite: *Forest on the banks of the Rungan River near Palangkaraya, Central Kalimantan. This region of Borneo consists of extensive, low-lying and rather swampy plains, some sandy, some peaty, with forests of generally short stature.*

Below: *One of the numerous channels in the floodplain of the mighty Barito River, South Kalimantan, south of Banjarmasin. Water levels vary with tide and rainfall.*

Above: *Patches of permanently waterlogged ground like this are common in the coastal zone of southern Borneo. They are characteristically covered in thick shrubby vegetation, but taller trees will not grow here.*

Opposite: *The Sekunir River flows through Tanjung Puting National Park in Central Kalimantan. River boats remain the most important means of transport through much of southern Borneo, where they are known as klotok. The forests along the banks of the Sekunir are an important habitat for the remarkable, long-nosed Proboscis Monkey.*

Right: *A wild bilberry* (Vaccinium *species*) *beside the Sekunir River in Tanjung Puting National Park.*

THE PEOPLE

People have lived on Borneo for at least 40,000 years, and today's varied population embraces many languages, cultures, lifestyles and religions. Such diversity is the result of centuries of shifting settlements and interminglings, trade and immigration from other parts of Asia. The lives of the different peoples have also been shaped by the varied profile of the land itself.

The Muslim communities of the coastal regions, who make up about two-thirds of the total population, have a mixed ancestry of indigenous groups and settlers from elsewhere in Asia. Some groups are traditionally traders, others fishermen, yet others farmers, while a few are craftsmen. Some live in extensive villages built on stilts over the sea, others on riverside terraces or coastal plains. In recent years, many have moved permanently to towns. Though most see themselves primarily as Malays, some groups take a pride in their distinct cultural identity. The Brunei Malays, for example, have their origins in the earliest centre of trade between Borneo and China, already thriving over a thousand years ago. Though trade with China is of such long standing, significant Chinese settlement in Borneo began only around 1750. The Chinese are prominent in the fields of trade and commerce: the urban centres of Sarawak and Sabah remain largely Chinese strongholds.

The inland farmers – the Iban and Bidayuh of Sarawak, the Kayan Kenyah and Kelabit-Lun-Bawang of the central highlands, the Maloh of West Kalimantan, the scattered Barito of the south, the Dusun-Kadazan-Murut group of Sabah – originally settled along the rivers that gave them access to the interior of Borneo, building communal longhouses which are still central to the culture of some peoples. Many of their traditions remain alive, including their religions, which hinge on a belief in a supernatural world of good and evil spirits. Their shifting cultivation of rice and harvesting of forest produce means that their lives are wedded to the forest.

Above: *A longhouse at Mancong Village, Tanjung Isuy, East Kalimantan. Although this longhouse was constructed for visitors and tourists, the carving and joinery seen here illustrate the traditional importance of wood to the various Dayak communities of southern Borneo. At the entrance (opposite) the central item is the traditional form of access ladder to a longhouse, made by carving notches into an ironwood pole.*

PREVIOUS PAGES
Page 100. Above left: *Kelabit woman at Bario, Sarawak. She has a multipurpose basket, made from woven rattan and supported by a head strap, used for carrying all manner of items such as farm tools or produce.*
Above right: *A typical market stall scene over the Brunei River at Bandar Seri Begawan, Brunei. Older women and elderly men, who leave younger folk to engage in more strenuous tasks, contribute to the family economy by selling fruit and vegetable produce from their gardens.*
Below left: *Bajau buffalo farmers at the weekly* tamu *(market), Kota Belud, western Sabah.*
Below right: *Bugis mother with her infant, sleeping soundly in a cloth sarong suspended from a beam in a riverboat 'taxi', on the Mahakam River, East Kalimantan.*
Page 101: *Firewood seller at Banjarmasin, the riverine capital of South Kalimantan.*

Above: *A communal rice barn in the Longnawan region of East Kalimantan. Raised on stilts, it is decorated in typical Kenyah style.*

Many aspects of traditional culture are kept alive throughout Borneo. Above left: *A Dayak dancer performs at a festival in Kuching, wearing a mix of modern and traditional clothing.* Above: *Silver jewellery, heirlooms of an Iban family in Sarawak.* Below left: *Iban festival at Pyot longhouse, near Marudi, Sarawak. Traditional brass gongs and mats of woven plant fibre have been brought out for the occasion.* Opposite: *Young Iban women at a longhouse in the Limbang area, northern Sarawak, wearing traditional silver jewellery, bright modern beadware based on traditional Iban motifs, and colourful sarongs that might belong to any race or period in Borneo.*

PREVIOUS PAGES
A village near Tanjung Isuy, Mahakam River, East Kalimantan. The inhabitants have chosen to live in individual family houses rather than the traditional longhouse. Even so, their homes are still built using traditional materials and styles, such as the ironwood shingles and the raised platforms on which the houses are constructed. The waterway has many different functions in the lives of the villagers; they travel along it by dug-out canoe to reach the main river, and use it for bathing and laundry.

Above: *Iban longhouse on the Rajang River. The design and location – well above maximum flood level – are traditional. As in many parts of northern and western Borneo, however, the roof is of corrugated metal rather than the ironwood shingles or palm thatch which would have been used in earlier times.*

Left: *An Iban man of the Rajang River, in Kapit. Lean and active, taking pride in his tattoos, he has stopped outside a shop to chew betel-nut (a freshly prepared mixture of betel-pepper leaf, Areca palm seed, and lime).*

Above: *Iban youngsters at Pyot longhouse near Marudi, Sarawak. Like those throughout most of Borneo, they attend school and will have the choice of staying in a rural community or moving to an urban or industrial livelihood, perhaps elsewhere within Sarawak or even in Peninsular Malaysia.*

Right: *An Iban family in Kapit, Sarawak. They have come from their longhouse to purchase supplies such as kerosene, matches, soap, sugar and salt.*

Bario (opposite, above) *is the largest of several old settlements of the Kelabit people of northern Sarawak. The area is one of extensive irrigated rice fields, farmhouses, and central community buildings. The stability of the Kelabit community is reflected in the harmonious group of three generations* (above).

Opposite, below: *As in many parts of Borneo, headdress provides the opportunity for people to retain traditional fashions and motifs even though these Kelabits' everyday clothing might be found anywhere in the world. The man's cap* (near left) *incorporates hornbill feathers and Clouded Leopard teeth.*

Right: *The headman and his wife at their hearth in Long Dano longhouse, Kelabit Highlands.*

Scenes from a Kenyah village near Longnawan, East Kalimantan. Above: *A bridge across the river, made entirely of bamboo stems lashed together with rattan cord.* Right: *Cooking rice – the staple food for most Bornean communities.*

Opposite: *A Penan child at a settlement near Gunung Mulu, Sarawak. Traditionally nomadic, living entirely off the forest, the majority of Penan communities are now settled farmers.*

Above: *Kampung Air, the water village at Bandar Seri Begawan, Brunei, is actually composed of about forty sections, each with its own headman. The largest Brunei Malay community in Borneo is concentrated here, as it was in 1521 when the Italian chronicler of Magellan's fleet sailed into Brunei Bay.*

Left: *The Omar Ali Saifuddin Mosque, built in 1958, seen from Kampung Air.*

Above: *A resident's view of Kampung Air. It is possible to move about through the water village using a combination of plank walkways and boat taxis. The stilt houses are supplied with electricity and water from the mainland, but the Brunei government is encouraging residents to apply for houses in resettlement schemes on land.*

Right: *Fishing nets at Kampung Air.*

In addition to Bandar Seri Begawan, most coastal zone communities in Borneo either consist of or incorporate a water village. The largest of these is at Banjarmasin, South Kalimantan, with its 'floating market' (opposite). At Banjarmasin, the Barito River, subject to tidal influence, is the place where washing and food preparation are done (above).

Right: Young Malay women being ferried across the river at Bako village, on the Sarawak coast near Kuching – a typical scene in a land where rivers provide the focal points for so many communities.

Rice cultivation forms the basis of the traditional economy for most inland peoples in Borneo, in a wide variety of situations and landscapes. Above: Tambunan Valley, Sabah, home of the Tambunan Dusuns, lies at about 550 metres (1,800 feet) above sea level and is surrounded by the Crocker Range and the Trus Madi Range of mountains (far distance). Wet rice is grown on the fertile valley alluvium, while hill rice, bamboo groves, orchards and secondary forests cover the nearby foothills. Left: A Bidayuh hill rice farm in the undulating lowlands of southern Sarawak. The house is a temporary structure, and its main purpose is to permit the ripening crop to be guarded constantly against the depredations of seed-eating munia birds which would otherwise be capable of wiping out the entire crop. Secondary forest has been retained nearby, allowing tree seeds to recolonize the rice fields after they have been abandoned. Maintenance of fallow land under forest is the basis of swidden farming (stable shifting cultivation) in most parts of Borneo.

Opposite, above: Illanun dwellings of poles and Nipa palm thatch, on the sandy coastal Tempasuk Plain, western Sabah. The crops grown here include dry rice and corn. The open grassland of the plain is maintained by grazing animals and fire. The soil, inherently infertile, is manured by herds of buffalo, cattle and horses. Below: On the more fertile, clayey inland edge of Tempasuk Plain, Dusun farming communities plant wet rice. Here, young people cooperate to gather in the rice crop.

Gunung Kinabalu, here viewed from the Tempasuk Plain, is important in various ways to the people of Sabah. In times past, surrounding Dusun communities are believed to have regarded the summit as the resting-place of the spirits of their ancestors. Nowadays, some of the same communities earn a handsome living planting vegetables on the middle slopes of the south side of the mountain. For some lowland communities, Kinabalu is an essential source of fresh water.

Regular markets, daily, weekly, monthly or annual, where all manner of goods are sold, are a feature of many parts of Borneo. The Kota Belud market in Sabah (above) *is held every Sunday.*

Below: *In some coastal parts of Borneo, notably northern Sarawak and south-western Sabah, the swamp sago palm* (Metroxylon sagu) *is traditionally the prime source of dietary carbohydrate. The palm is felled just before it flowers, when the trunk is rich in starch. The trunk is then cut into pieces, pulverized, and shaken in running water. The water is captured and the starch extracted. Here, a Bisaya man is extracting sago starch under the shade of his rubber tree plantation.*

Freshwater rivers and lakes represent an important source of fish to some Bornean communities. Above: A fisherman's house on the Kahayan River, Central Kalimantan. Left: An Orang Sungai family inspect their net, set across an oxbow lake off the Kinabatangan River, eastern Sabah. This particular lake is situated within a rattan plantation, developed by the government of Sabah. The rattan is planted in regenerating logged secondary forests, thereby supporting forest conservation and protection of the fisheries from less benign forms of land use.

Above: *A fisherman on the massive, shallow Semayang lake off the Mahakam River, East Kalimantan. A variety of methods are used to obtain freshwater fish in Borneo. Nets may be set between poles, as here, at the mouth of a tributary entering a lake or river, or across a stream. Casting nets are also often used in shallow waters. Natural plant toxins may be used in some circumstances to stupefy fish which are scooped from the water by hand or with small nets. Hooks and lines are widely used to catch large fish.*

Right: *A Selakau man (one of the Bidayuh group) at the Pueh longhouse, Sarawak, making a fish trap out of rattan. Such traps are typically set along riverbanks. Similar traps, baited with coconut pieces, are also set along the lower reaches of rivers to catch freshwater prawns.*

In terms of volume of catch and the number of people involved full-time, marine fisheries are even more important than freshwater fisheries in Borneo. Many marine fish species depend on either mangrove forests or coral reefs for shelter and as feeding-grounds, especially in the early phases of their life-cycle. The destruction of mangrove reduces the productivity of marine fisheries. In some areas, fish are obtained with underwater bombs. This highly damaging method of fishing has destroyed some coral reefs off northern Borneo. Above: *Fishermen selling their catch at Bandar Seri Begawan, Brunei.* Opposite: *Fishing boats off Kota Kinabalu, capital of Sabah.* Right: *A basket of sea produce at Kota Kinabalu wharf.*

Above: *The Sarawak River at Kuching, the capital of Sarawak. Though a fast developing modern city, Kuching retains the flavour of its colonial past as the seat of power of the 'White Rajahs'.*

Left: *A fishing boat on the Sarawak River.*

Above: *Like all larger towns in Sarawak and Sabah, Sibu evolved around a settlement of ethnic Chinese traders and its population is still largely Chinese. Its situation on the Rajang River, which is navigable by large boats, has enabled Sibu to become a major port, and it is the centre of the Sarawak timber industry.*

Right: *River boats at Kapit, Rajang River. The long, covered passenger boats are the riverine equivalent of express buses.*

Forest products were once a very significant element in the economy of most indigenous peoples and the main reason for Chinese traders to visit Borneo. Apart from timber and rattan, the volume of trade in forest products has declined greatly. For some people, however, harvesting or selling forest products remains a part of their livelihood. Left: *Wild honey-bee nests in a Mengaris (Koompassia excelsa) tree. Two centuries ago, the wax from these nests, used to make candles, was a major trade item from Bornean forests. Now, the wax has little value but the honey is popular locally.* Below left: *A Kadazan woman sells wild honey and a variety of fruits on a street corner in Kota Kinabalu, Sabah.* Below centre: *A Selakau man in south-western Sarawak displays his collection of Engkabang nuts (seeds of the dipterocarp tree Shorea macrophylla), which yield a viscous edible oil.* Below right: *Kelabit hunters near Bario, Sarawak, seek Bearded Pigs and deer with the aid of their sturdy hunting dogs.*

Opposite: *Harvesting of edible birds' nests made by some species of swiftlets using rattan ladders and ropes in Gomantong caves, Sabah. The produce derived from this precarious occupation is made into birds' nest soup, a delicacy to the Chinese.*

Above: *Pearls, harvested from wild oysters by Bajau divers, were once one of the more valuable trade items from the coastal zone of north-eastern Borneo. Pearl culture farms – such as the one shown here – offer a modern alternative.*

Left: *The Estuarine Crocodile* (Crocodylus porosus) *occurs in the larger rivers and coastal regions of Borneo. Several crocodile 'farms' have been established, such as this one at Sandakan, Sabah. The workers displaying the skins are from Timor in Indonesia. The supple skin of the crocodile's belly is exported for the manufacture of handbags Bond footwear.*

Two centuries ago, the presence of gold in south-western Borneo and diamonds in the south-east was one of the factors which attracted Chinese settlers and foreign traders to the island. Nowadays, Borneo is only a minor producer of precious stones and metals. Apart from a copper mine in Sabah and coal mines in Kalimantan, most current mining activities in Borneo are small-scale and labour-intensive. Above: *Digging for diamonds in the Cempaka area near Banjarmasin, South Kalimantan.* Right: *Panning for gold near Tanjung Puting National Park, Central Kalimantan.*

Logging of the natural forests of Borneo, for the supply of large quantities of commercial timber for export, has had a major impact on the landscape in recent decades. Much of the dipterocarp forest has now been logged, particularly in the lowlands. Old logging trails permeate the forests creating a giant patchwork of forested blocks. However, commercial logging does not mean deforestation. The key steps involved in logging are planning and construction of a road system (above), felling of large trees (centre left) – between 5 to 15 per hectare (10 to 35 per acre) in most cases – and mechanical extraction of the tree trunks, usually with bulldozer-type tractors, but in some cases with the use of long steel cables from the road or even by helicopter. The trunks are cut into sections at 'landing' points and taken out of the forest by lorry (below left). In some cases, the lorries transport the logs directly to a mill or to the coast for export. Often, the logs are taken to a large river and floated to the coast. A variable percentage of the forest is damaged during logging operations, depending on the abundance of commercial trees and on the amount of care taken by the loggers. After logging operations have stopped, the forest is left to regenerate naturally from young trees, saplings and seedlings.

Wherever possible, rivers are used to transport logs from logging areas to the coast and to wood-processing mills, because transportation by river is normally cheaper than by road. Above: *Logs being towed down the Baram River, Sarawak. Many tropical hardwood species are heavier than water and have to be carried on barges.* Right: *A plywood factory on the bank of the Barito River, South Kalimantan.*

Traditional farming and commercial logging have been blamed for 'deforestation' in Borneo. Rather, the conversion of forests to other forms of land use has been and continues to be the basic reason for loss of natural forests.

Opposite: *This area in eastern Sabah was logged in the 1970s and burned during the 1983 drought. It has since been allocated by the government for permanent agriculture, a public road has been built and titles issued to landowners. They will sell any remaining timber, and plant crops such as oil palm.*

Above right: *A plantation of Batai trees* (Paraserianthes falcataria), *a fast-growing species developed for wood production. Roughly every fifteen years, all trees are felled and a new crop is planted.*

Centre right: *An oil palm plantation with palms between one and two years old. The oil palm, a native of West Africa, is an ideal crop for Borneo because it can tolerate a variety of soil conditions and thrives on heavy rainfall. The oils that its fruits yield are used for a variety of products, notably for edible oils and soaps.*

Below: *In some areas, traditional farming is combined with plantation crops. This aerial view, near Samunsam Wildlife Sanctuary in Sarawak, shows pepper gardens (note the regular spacing) mixed with vegetable gardens, rice fields, orchards and land under forest fallow.*

FOLLOWING PAGES
Bugis schooners at Banjarmasin, South Kalimantan. From their homelands in southern Sulawesi, the Muslim Bugis people emerged in early historic times as the greatest indigenous seafarers and traders of the South-east Asian archipelago. There are now many Bugis communities in Borneo.

135

THE WILDLIFE

The wildlife of Borneo is characterized by subtlety and, with a few notable exceptions, smallness of size. The wonder of the island's animal life lies not in great spectacles of a few species but in an enormous diversity of forms. Patience is needed to experience Borneo's wildlife. Listening is as rewarding as looking. Often, signs of animals – footprints, nests, remains of food – are more readily seen than their makers.

Rainforest mammals range from the tiny Least Woolly Bat to the Asian Elephant. Orang-utans and other primates inhabit many parts of the island, although some species are declining as their habitats diminish. Walking in dense rainforest is not easy, while climbing through the trees can be dangerous and uses a lot of precious energy. Perhaps this explains why nearly half the mammals of Borneo – bats, flying squirrels and Colugo – can fly or glide.

Over two hundred kinds of birds are found in an average piece of lowland dipterocarp forest. Most are usually heard rather than seen, but a keen bird-watcher armed with binoculars can spot dozens of species within a few days.

Rainforest insects outnumber the mammals and birds by thousands to one, their combined humming, buzzes and clicks making a giant engine of the forest. Other creepy-crawlies are varied – encompassing spiders, centipedes, scorpions and snakes – but discreet and mostly harmless. Indeed, the array of wildlife in Borneo is remarkably harmless to people and even disease-bearing life forms are generally less nasty than in most other equatorial regions.

Colourful fish, turtles and dolphins inhabit the open seas around Borneo, and some species enter the coastal mangrove forests to shelter or feed. It is the spectacular coral reefs, however, which are home to the richest marine wildlife, rivalling the rainforests in variety and intricacy.

Opposite: *Wild elephants* (Elephas maximus), *seen here feeding in secondary forest near the Kinabatangan River, in Sabah, are to be found only in the lowland forests of the north-eastern tip of Borneo. They are very selective eaters, preferring grasses, young palm shoots, wild bananas and gingers. The small herds consist of several females and their young, while adult males are usually solitary.*

Orang-utans occur only in northern Sumatra and scattered parts of Borneo, mostly in lowland and swamp forests. Above: Male Orang-utan at Sepilok Forest Reserve, Sabah. Below: Mother and infant at Tanjung Puting National Park, Central Kalimantan.

PREVIOUS PAGES
Page 138. *Above left: Rhinoceros Hornbill* (Buceros rhinoceros), *the State bird of Sarawak, where it is called* kenyalang. *Above right: A hemipteran bug at Kutai, East Kalimantan. Most bugs suck juices from plants and some emit a strong odour if disturbed. Below left: One of a variety of shell-less molluscs called nudibranches, which dwell on coral reefs around Borneo. Below right: Baby Orang-utan* (Pongo pygmaeus) *at Tanjung Puting National Park, Central Kalimantan.*

Page 139: *Rajah Brooke's Birdwing butterfly* (Trogonoptera brookiana), *a scarce and handsome species with a wing span of up to 17 centimetres (7 inches).*

Forest clearance for agriculture in the fertile lowlands of eastern Borneo has displaced many Orang-utans. This trend is continuing. Some individuals affected in this way are caught by wildlife and conservation authorities, and taken to protected forests elsewhere. Mature Orang-utans are expected to fend for themselves but young individuals – like these at Tanjung Puting, Kalimantan (above left and left) – have to be provided with food and shelter, and encouraged to learn to survive on their own.

Above right: *An adult Orang-utan weaves together leafy twigs and branches in the forest canopy to make a springy sleeping-nest. A fresh platform is constructed every day.*

Gibbons are slender, acrobatic apes of the South-east Asian rainforests. They are a prominent feature of the hill and lowland forests of Borneo, where two species are found. Unusually amongst mammals, gibbons live in small, stable groups of one adult male, one adult female and between one and three youngsters. The adult pair indulges in singing loud duets, and the call of the female carries over long distances. A gibbon moves rapidly through the forest, its body suspended like a pendulum from its long arms. It feeds on ripe fruits, leaf shoots and insects.

Above: *Agile Gibbon* (Hylobates agilis), *a species found between the Barito and Kapuas rivers in Kalimantan.*

Right: *Bornean Gibbon* (Hylobates muelleri), *which occurs in the remainder of Borneo.*

Macaques are adaptable, social monkeys that live in groups of twenty or more. Two species are widely distributed through Borneo. Both species dwell in forests but commonly come out into plantations and rural gardens, where they raid fruit trees. Above: *The Pig-tailed Macaque* (Macaca nemestrina) *is a creature of hill forests, living in wide-ranging groups that travel both through the trees and on the ground.* Left: *The Long-tailed Macaque* (Macaca fascicularis) *is a native of coastal and lowland forests. It is often seen on the banks of large rivers. In coastal mangroves, this monkey will feed on crabs.*

The Proboscis Monkey (Nasalis larvatus) is confined to Borneo, and breeding populations occur only in parts of the coastal zone and along some large rivers. The distinctive feature of this monkey is the nose, long and pendulous in mature males (above), short and snub-like in females and young (right). Proboscis Monkeys can be seen most readily from a boat, in riverine forests and mangroves. Every afternoon, groups congregate in trees along watercourses, where they pass the night perched precariously next to the water. Early in the morning, they move away into the forest where they spend the day. These gentle monkeys feed predominantly on the leaves and seeds of a variety of trees.

Above: *Female Sambar Deer* (Cervus unicolor), *the largest deer species in Borneo.* Right: *Greater Mouse-deer* (Tragulus napu), *a diminutive animal which feeds on fallen fruits and vegetation in shady parts of the forest.*

Opposite, far left: *Colugo or Flying Lemur* (Cynocephalus variegatus), *a strange gliding mammal with no close living relatives.* Above left: *Slow Loris* (Nycticebus coucang), *a nocturnal relative of the monkeys.* Below left: *Sun Bear* (Helarctos malayanus), *also known as the Honey Bear. The smallest of the world's bears, it feeds mainly on termites, grubs and the contents of bees' nests.*

147

Borneo has a wide variety of birds, some resident and some seasonal migrants from northern Asia. Opposite: Wreathed Hornbill (Rhyticeros undulatus), *one of eight species of hornbills found in Borneo. This species is common in some localities where there is extensive tall forest cover, such as Tabin Wildlife Reserve in Sabah. It has a call rather like the yelp of a small dog. Large hornbills have distinctive wing-beats, reminding some listeners of a small steam train. Right:* Pied Hornbill (Anthracoceros convexus), *a species confined to riverine forests in the lowlands. It has a noisy, cackling call. Below:* Blue-throated Bee-eater (Merops viridis), *a migrant species most often seen in open coastal plains.*

Above: *Young White-bellied Sea-eagle* (Haliaeetus leucogaster), *a resident of the coastal zone. This magnificent bird, with a mighty wingspan, can be seen soaring above the sea off coastal towns and above cliffs. Its call is a series of loud, goose-like quacks.*

Left: *The Brahminy Kite* (Haliastur indus), *considered sacred by the Iban, is one of the most familiar birds of prey in Borneo, generally seen over open country and settlements in the coastal regions. Its call is a harsh meeow.*

Opposite: *Heron in a riverside tree, Sekunir River, Central Kalimantan.*

Above left: *Blue-eared Kingfisher* (Alcedo meninting), *a resident of forest streams and one of eleven species of kingfishers occurring in Borneo.*

Above right: *Emerald Dove* (Chalcophaps indica), *a quiet, usually solitary bird that keeps to the ground under low tree cover. From time to time, large numbers migrate from one area to another.*

Left: *Male Crestless Fireback Pheasant* (Lophura erythropthalma), *a forest-dwelling bird of Brunei, Sarawak and western Kalimantan. The male (shown here) makes distinctive whirring sounds with its wings.*

Above: *Malayan Night-heron* (Gorsachius melanolophus), *also known as the Tiger Bittern, a rarely-seen bird of dense vegetation cover in swamps.*

Right: *Male Blue-headed Pitta* (Pitta baudii), *a beautiful bird confined to Borneo. It favours damp, shady spots in lowland dipterocarp forests.*

Left: *White-breasted Waterhen* (Amaurornis phoenicurus), *a bird of almost every type of habitat other than forest. Wherever there is damp, tall grassy cover, this species is almost certain to be found. It utters a variety of noisy calls.*

Below left: *Male Asian Fairy Bluebird* (Irena puella). *This attractive bird occurs in most lowland areas where there is extensive tree cover. It feeds on fruits and insects.*

Opposite: *Lesser Adjutant Stork* (Leptoptilos javanicus), *a massively built bird which feeds on carrion and fish. Although scarce, it can be found in many parts of Borneo. It is most often seen in extensive open coastal wetlands.*

Above: *The Estuarine Crocodile (Crocodylus porosus) is the largest reptile in Borneo, growing to nearly 6 metres (20 feet) in length. The species occurs mainly in the lower reaches of large rivers and in mangroves. In the 19th century, the Estuarine Crocodile was considered a serious threat to people living along Bornean rivers. After decades of intensive hunting, numbers are now very much reduced and there are only occasional incidents of people being killed.*

There are over 150 species of snakes in Borneo and the great majority are non-poisonous. Almost all snakes are shy, retiring creatures. Centre left: Yellow-ringed Cat-snake (Boiga dendrophila), a fearsome-looking but harmless creature most often found in the mangrove zone. Below left: Grey-tailed Racer Snake (Gonyosoma oxycephalum), Pulau Tiga Park, Sabah.

Opposite: Water Monitor (Varanus salvator), Borneo's largest lizard, enjoying the sun in a tree on the banks of the Sekunir River, Central Kalimantan.

Above: *A ground-dwelling frog* (Pedostibes hosei) *in Gunung Mulu National Park, Sarawak.*

Right: *Crested Lizard* (Calotes cristatellus), *a species of forest edges. This lizard can change its skin from bright green to a dull brownish colour.*

Opposite, above left: *A tree frog* (Polypedates otilophus), *a native of low, bushy areas near streams and other damp areas.*

Below left: *Gliding Lizards* (Draco *species*) *in swamp forest, Kinabatangan, Sabah. These small lizards are characterized by the small flaps of skin along each side of their body, which can be stretched, allowing them to glide between tree trunks. Here, a male, with yellow and white throat flag, also formed by means of an extensible flap of skin, is displaying to a female.*

Borneo's butterflies are spectacular and beautiful but their appearances are seasonal: some species are abundant at certain times of the year but disappear completely in other months. Opposite: *Butterfly of the family Nymphalidae, in Kutai National Park, Kalimantan.* Right: *Five-barred Swallowtail* (Graphium antiphates itamputi). Below: *Four beautiful species of butterflies, all males, feeding on the minerals in an animal dropping on the forest floor near Bario, Sarawak. The one at the top of the picture with red and yellow markings is the Glorious Begum* (Agatasa calydonia). *The others (clockwise) are a Nawab* (Polyura *species), a Sergeant* (Athyma *species) and a Blue Nawab* (Polyura schreiber).

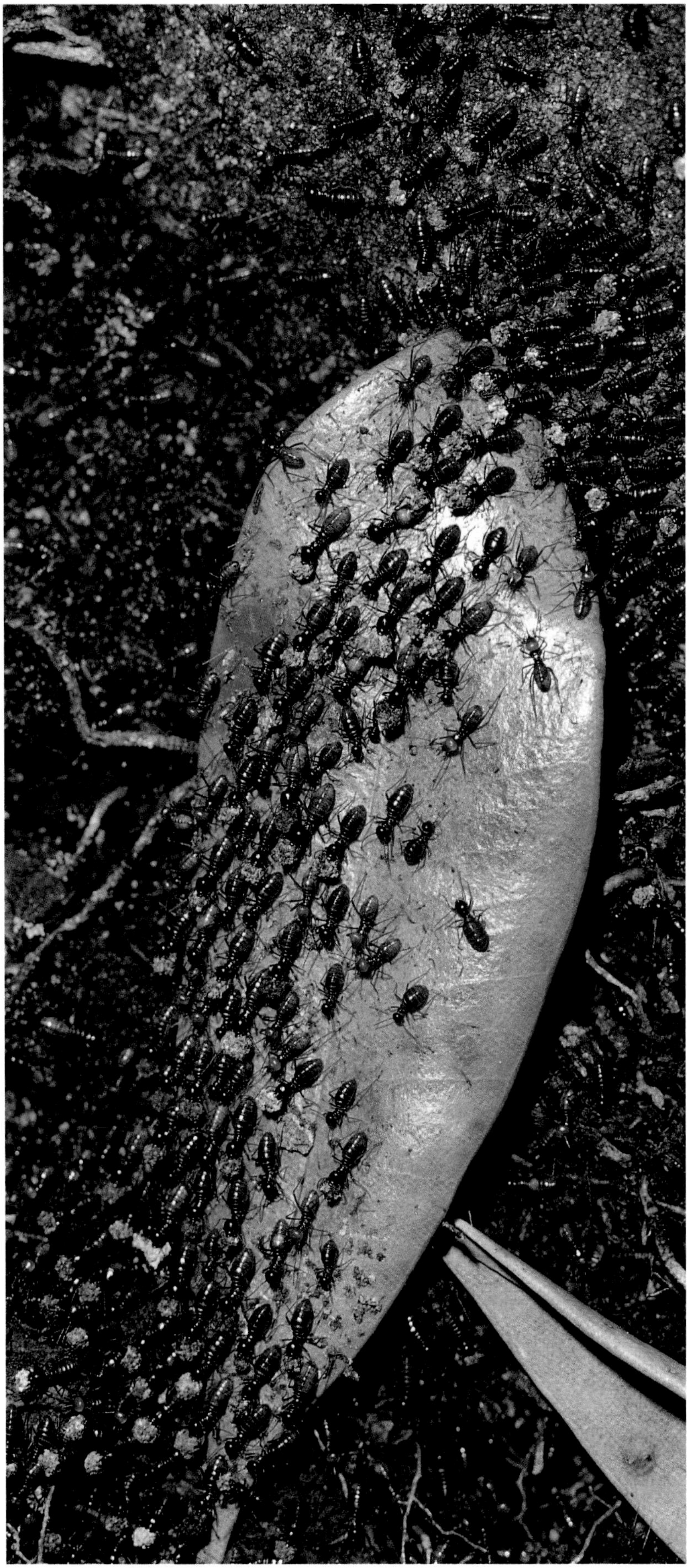

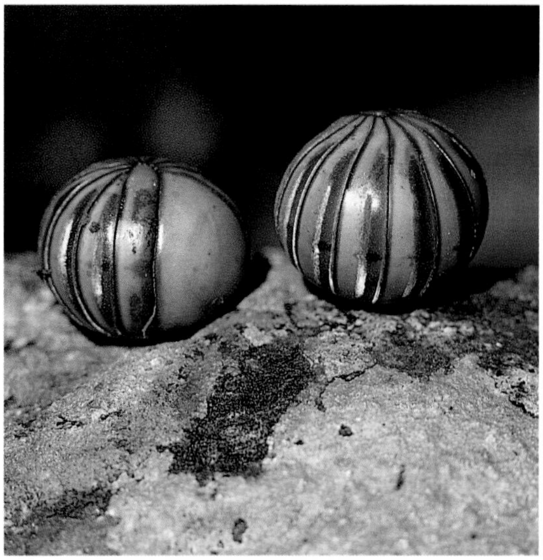

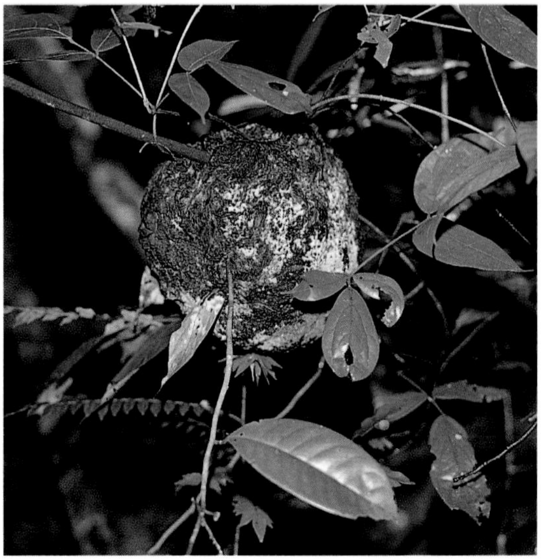

Left: *Termites represent one of the most abundant and ecologically important groups of insects in the Bornean rainforest. They can burrow into and digest wood. This community of* Hospitalitermes *termites is on the move across the forest floor, many individuals loaded with wood for nest-building.* Top: *Large pill millipedes (order* Oniscomorpha*) live in the leaf litter of the Bornean rainforest floor, feeding on decaying vegetation. They roll up, like this, when threatened with danger.* Above: *Ants are also very abundant in the rainforest. This ants' nest is attached to saplings, and constructed from plant material chewed to a pulp by the ants.* Opposite: *This stunning picture of a handsome grasshopper belies the fact that it can be a very serious pest, feeding in massive swarms on the leaf blades of young rice plants. Along with seed-eating munia birds it is one of the most feared creatures in traditional rice-growing communities.*

Above: *A damselfly. The delicate relatives of the dragonflies, with a more fluttering manner of flight, damselflies rely on their powerful vision to hunt and catch their prey on the wing.*

Right: *Female spiny-backed spider (family Argiopidae), well protected from predation by birds. The brilliant yellowish colouring probably serves as a warning against tackling the sharp spines.*

Below right: *The predatory assassin bug (family Reduviidae) hunts on the ground, feeding on other insects by sucking out their body fluids through puncture wounds.*

Opposite: *A group of heteropteran shield bugs (Catacanthus incarnatus), so named because of the shield-like form of the body. Most forest bugs feed on the sap of plants.*

The tiny island of Sipadan, south of Sabah's Semporna Peninsula, is one of the world's richest dive sites. The coral reef can be explored both under clear shallow water and on the reef wall where the sea-bed drops away to a depth of 600 metres (2,000 feet). The Gorgonian Sea Fan (above) is to be found in deeper waters. Anchored amongst a variety of corals, its arms extend into the current to trap small creatures swept past it.

Left: The Tomato Clownfish (Premnas biaculeatus), found in shallow waters, lives in the shelter of a sea anemone. The fish is protected from the anemone's sting by a special coating of mucus on its skin.

Both the Hawksbill Turtle (Eretmochelys imbricata) *(above) and the larger Green Turtle* (Chelonia mydas) *(right) are found off the northeast coast of Sabah. All marine turtle species are endangered: their numbers have fallen dangerously low through the collection of their eggs, and they are frequently drowned when accidentally caught in fishing nets and traps. The Green Turtle is widely hunted for its meat while the Hawksbill's carapace is the source of tortoiseshell. Strategies to build up turtle populations include the protection of nesting beaches, and the development of turtle hatcheries, where the eggs are protected from land predators as well as egg-collectors.*

The warm shallow waters of the coral reef teem with life, and the biological diversity of this marine environment rivals that of the rainforest. Left: *A shoal of Yellow Lined Emperors* (Gnathodentex aureolineatus) *accompanied by Yellow-fin Goat Fish* (Mulliodes vanicolensis). *The cuttlefish* (above) *is able to escape detection by predators – and prey – by adjusting its coloration to match its background.*

Above: *Clown Triggerfish* (Balistoides conspiculum). *About 50 centimetres (18 inches) long, its name refers to its first dorsal spine which it is able to erect and lock in position. When the fish wedges itself into a crevice for protection, the spine prevents it from being pulled out by a predator.*

Left: *Leaf fish, like this pink one, are predatory and though small, their large mouths enable them to eat creatures almost their own size. They prefer slow or still water near the shore, where they may drift like a dead leaf until they sight their prey.*

170

Above: *Yellow-faced Angelfish* (Pomacanthus xanthometopon). *These beautiful shy fish remain close to the coral so that they can dart into a crevice if danger threatens.*

Right: *Nudibranches like this* Chromodoris bullocki *vary widely in their coloration. A form of sea slug, their name refers to their naked dorsal gills. This one has settled on a sea squirt* (Polycarpa aurata) *whose body consists mostly of a hugely developed pharynx through which it both feeds and breathes.*

CONSERVATION AREAS IN BORNEO

The only way in which most wild species of plants and animals can be conserved in perpetuity is to protect an array of all their natural habitats, in the form of Parks, Reserves and Sanctuaries established by law. The following lists summarise some of the main conservation areas which are either already established or in the process of being established in Borneo. Many other areas which are important for the conservation of wild species are omitted from the lists, because they have been established primarily for water catchment protection, timber production, human community use, recreation, education or research, and because there are too many to list in full. The lists below include those areas of particular interest or importance, and those which are most accessible to visitors (marked *).

ha. = hectares (1 hectare = 2.47 acres)

SABAH

CROCKER RANGE NATIONAL PARK* (139,919 ha.). Long mountain range, important for water catchment protection.

DANUM VALLEY CONSERVATION AREA* (42,755 ha.). A diversity of dipterocarp forests. Location of a Field Studies Centre.

GOMANTONG FOREST RESERVE* (3,297 ha.). Limestone hill with edible birds' nest caves.

KINABALU PARK* (75,370 ha.). Location of Gunung Kinabalu, South-east Asia's highest mountain.

KINABATANGAN WILDLIFE SANCTUARY* (in process of establishment). Proboscis Monkeys and many other mammals and birds. Riverine and lake habitats.

GUNUNG SILAM* (4,128 ha.). Small coastal mountain of ultrabasic rock, with unusual flora.

RAFFLESIA VIRGIN JUNGLE RESERVE* (356 ha.). The most accessible *Rafflesia* flower site in Borneo.

SEMPORNA MARINE PARK* (in process of establishment). Scenic coral reefs and island habitats.

SEPILOK FOREST RESERVE* (4,292 ha.). Location of Borneo's oldest Orang-utan rehabilitation centre.

TABIN WILDLIFE RESERVE (122,530 ha.). Important area for large mammals.

TAWAU HILLS PARK (27,972 ha.). Fine dipterocarp forests. Important for water catchment protection.

TUNKU ABDUL RAHMAN PARK* (islands and sea: 4,929 ha.). Corals and forests. Very near to Kota Kinabalu.

TURTLE ISLANDS PARK* (islands and sea: 1,740 ha.). Important nesting site for Green Turtles.

SARAWAK

BAKO NATIONAL PARK* (2,728 ha.). Coastal cliffs and heath forest habitats.

BATANG AI NATIONAL PARK* (24,040 ha.). Water catchment area for hydro-power dam. Adjacent to Lanjak-Entimau Wildlife Sanctuary.

GUNUNG GADING NATIONAL PARK* (4,196 ha.). Contains *Rafflesia tuan-mudae*.

GUNUNG MULU NATIONAL PARK* (52,887 ha.). Massive cave systems and a variety of species-rich forest habitats.

LAMBIR HILLS NATIONAL PARK* (6,952 ha.). Diverse dipterocarp flora on low sandstone hills.

LANJAK-ENTIMAU WILDLIFE SANCTUARY (168,755 ha.). Remote dipterocarp forests. Main Orang-utan sanctuary in Sarawak.

LOAGAN BUNUT NATIONAL PARK (10,245 ha.). Peat swamp and lake habitats, protecting both wildlife and traditional fishing activities.

NIAH NATIONAL PARK* (3,140 ha.). Borneo's prime archaeological site. Limestone outcrops and dipterocarp forest.

SIMILAJAU NATIONAL PARK (7,067 ha.). Coastal forest; sandy beaches.

BRUNEI DARUSSALAM

ULU TEMBURONG-BATU APOI FOREST RESERVE* (48,800 ha.). Hill dipterocarp forests. Location of Kuala Belalong Field Studies Centre.

WEST KALIMANTAN

DANAU SENTARUM RESERVE (80,000 ha.). A system of lakes surrounded by peat swamp forests.

GUNUNG BENTUANG-KARIMUN NATURE RESERVE (600,000 ha.). Extensive hill forests adjacent to Sarawak's Lanjak-Entimau Wildlife Sanctuary.

GUNUNG PALUNG NATURE RESERVE* (30,000 ha.). Contains an array of habitats from the coast up to 1,600 metres (5,250 feet) above sea level.

CENTRAL KALIMANTAN

BUKIT RAYA NATURE RESERVE (110,000 ha.). Contains Kalimantan's highest mountain peak.

PARARAWEN NATURE RESERVE (6,200 ha.). Remnant of undisturbed lowland dipterocarp forest.

TANJUNG PUTING NATIONAL PARK* (355,000 ha.). Extensive swamp, heath and lowland dipterocarp forests, with large populations of Orang-utans and Proboscis Monkeys.

SOUTH KALIMANTAN

PLEIHARI MARTAPURA GAME RESERVE (36,400 ha.). Botanically rich hill forests. The only extensive protected forest in south-east Borneo.

EAST KALIMANTAN

KUTAI NATIONAL PARK* (200,000 ha.). Lowland forests with large mammals. Suffered from fire in 1983.

SUNGAI KAYAN-MENTARANG NATURE RESERVE (1,600,000 ha.). The largest protected area in Borneo, containing a variety of forests and habitats, from riversides to mountains, bordering on to Sarawak and Sabah.

INDEX